Sensational Vancouver

by EVE LAZARUS

Sensational Vancouver

by EVE LAZARUS

anvil
PRESS

Anvil Press Publishers Inc.
P.O. Box 3008, Main Post Office
Vancouver, B.C. V6B 3X5 Canada
www.anvilpress.com

Library and Archives Canada Cataloguing in Publication

Lazarus, Eve, author
        Sensational Vancouver / Eve Lazarus.

Includes bibliographical references and index.
ISBN 978-1-927380-98-7 (pbk.)

        1. Celebrities--Homes and haunts--British Columbia--
Vancouver--History. 2. Celebrities--Homes and haunts--British
Columbia--Vancouver--Pictorial works. I. Title.

FC3847.25.L39 2014   971.1'33   C2014-900729-9

Book design: Derek von Essen
Cover concept: Rayola Graphic Design
Map: Ross Nelson

Cover photo credits:
Vancouver Skyline ca. 1962 Selwyn Pullan photo.
Joe Ricci (right) ca. 1950. Photo courtesy Louise Ricci.
West Coast Central Club ca. 1950. Photo courtesy Louise Ricci.
Tosca Trasolini, 1939. Photo courtesy Angela Stephens.
The Vogue Theatre, 2014. Derek von Essen photo.
6664 Marine Drive. Barry Downs Photo.
Back cover photo credit: BC Electric Head Office. Selwyn Pullan photo.

Represented in Canada by Publishers Group Canada.
Distributed in Canada by Raincoast and in the U.S. by Small Press Distribution (SPD).

The publisher gratefully acknowledges the financial assistance of the Canada Council for the Arts, the Canada Book Fund, and the Province of British Columbia through the B.C. Arts Council and the Book Publishing Tax Credit.

Printed and bound in Canada

FOR MIKE, MARK, MEGAN AND MATTHEW

ACKNOWLEDGEMENTS

While writing can be a solitary endeavour, I've been lucky to connect to an amazing group of people who share my love of history and have made the research, interviewing and writing even more fun.

My gratitude to John Belshaw, who took on 50,000 of my unedited words, beat them up and moulded them into a much better book. I would also like to thank Tom Carter, Aaron Chapman, Tom Hawthorn, James Johnstone, Lani Russwurm, Jason Vanderhill and Will Woods, who helped with leads and information and corrected my mistakes.

Thanks to Selwyn Pullan, whose wonderful 1962 photo of Vancouver is on the cover, and for the use of several other photos of architects and their buildings. Also thanks to Bryan Adams, Amber Bublé, Richard Bourgeois-Doyle, Barry Downs, Ken Dyck, Robert Karpa and Hans Sipma for the photos they contributed, Ross Nelson for the map, and especially Derek von Essen for his photos and the beautiful book design.

It would be impossible to write a history book without the resources of the archives, museums and public library. Special thanks to Megan Schlase at Vancouver Archives, to Kristin Hardie, curator at the Vancouver Police Museum, the staff at Vancouver Public Library's Special Collections, Sandra Boutilier at the Sun/ Province library, Lea Edgar at the Vancouver Maritime Museum, Eric L. Swanick, Special Collections, W.A.C. Bennett Library at Simon Fraser University, Kiriko Watanabe at the West Vancouver Museum, Janet Turner, archivist at North Vancouver Museum and Archives, the Oklahoma Historical Society, Kathryn Morrow and Jessica Quan at the Vancouver Heritage Foundation and my colleagues at the Vancouver Historical Society.

Thanks also to Gary Andolfatto, Greg Battle, William Dunn, John Stowe, Steve Webb and Elaine Willman for their time and expert assistance.

Thanks to the relatives and the dozens of homeowners, past and current, who shared their personal stories with me, loaned me photos from their family albums, and let me into their homes. For me, it's these personal stories and anecdotes that really make the houses and neighbourhoods of Vancouver come alive.

I'm especially grateful to my publisher Brian Kaufman for taking me on for a third book and to Karen Green and the staff at Anvil.

INTRODUCTION

When I write a history book there's always one character who really captures my attention. In *At Home with History* it was Alvo von Alvensleben. In *Sensational Victoria* it was Spoony Sundher. And, in *Sensational Vancouver*, it's Detective Joe Ricci, a kick-arse cop from the old school, who didn't get too hung up about warrants and other legal niceties. I got to know Joe through his daughter, who still lives in the house he built in 1922. Louise let me pour through boxes of news clippings and photographs and told me dozens of stories about her Dad. Joe was the first Italian to join the force. He was hired in 1912 because of his contacts within the close knit Italian community, his knowledge of the Black Hand (a sort of early version of the Mafia) and his ability, often with partner Donald Sinclair, to lock up the bad guys.

But while Ricci and Sinclair busted the opium dens, gambling joints and bootleggers, it was Lurancy Harris and Minnie Millar—the first female police officers in Canada—who patrolled the high-end brothels of Alexander Street. From all accounts Lurancy had an amazing career, retiring in 1928 with the rank of Inspector.

Vancouver in the first half of the 20th century was a seething mass of corruption. The top job at the Vancouver Police Department was a revolving door: the average tenure for a police chief was just four years. Police chiefs openly associated with criminals and Vancouver ran wild, headed up by a mayor elected for his "open town" policy. While East End families scraped through the Depression by selling cheap booze, the proceeds from US Prohibition made others rich, and produced some of the city's most iconic houses and buildings. The Marine Building, the Commodore Ballroom, The Vogue and several opulent houses in the city were built during the Depression from the proceeds of rum-running.

The second half of the 20th century also had egregious beginnings. Ray Munro's reporting brought down top cop Walter Mulligan, and newspapers captured every moment—from the Royal Commission into police corruption, to Mulligan's mistress, to the suicide of a police officer—in screaming headlines and detailed reporting that I've made much use of in these pages.

While Vancouver was still reeling from the Mulligan Affair, a series of brutal murders shocked the city. Around the same time, four newly minted police officers started stealing from Dairy Queens while they were on duty, escalated to bank robberies, and then nearly pulled off the heist of the century—$1.2 million in cancelled bank notes. On the eve of his arrest, one of the officers went home and murdered his wife and six children before turning the gun on himself.

But Vancouver is much more than crime. The city also produced some of the most amazing women you've likely never heard of: Elsie MacGill, Phyllis Munday, Nellie Yip Quong, Tosca Trasolini, Valerie Jerome and Joy Kogawa all lived or are still living sensational lives. Vancouver has a long tradition of sending off our talent to the rest of the world. A century of entertainment looks at stars like Yvonne DeCarlo, Mary Livingstone and more recently, Michael J. Fox, Bryan Adams and Michael Bublé, who came from modest beginnings and achieved international success.

Because the subtext of my books is about telling the stories behind our heritage buildings in order to save them, the final chapter is about the houses of mid-century architects. Ned Pratt, Barry Downs, Fred Hollingsworth and B.C. Binning designed modest, ground-breaking houses that they lived in all of their lives (Downs and Hollingsworth still do). Very few are left—most have been bulldozed in favour of huge mansions that impose their footprint on the landscape rather than become a part of it.

All of the homeowners I talked to, past and present, are fiercely proud of their homes. They are the custodians—sometimes for just a few years, others times for decades—who add their own stories to the homes and in turn play a vital part in the ongoing history of Sensational Vancouver.

—E.L., March 2014

CHAPTER 1

Joe Ricci's Vancouver

Detective Donald Sinclair brought the heavy axe down on the door. The wood splintered but wouldn't give. Like most of the opium dens along Shanghai Alley and in the rest of Chinatown, the door was iron-studded and made from heavy wood. As Sinclair and his partner Detective Joe Ricci had anticipated, the door was equipped with spring locking mechanisms typically found in opium dens and gambling joints.

Sinclair kept swinging the axe until he'd smashed through the door. The two detectives then raced down the narrow passageway and up three flights of stairs, battering their way through two more doors of similar strength. As they reached the fourth door, and the entrance to the smoking den, they could hear screams coming from the Chinese men locked inside.

In a frantic attempt to destroy the evidence, one of the men had pitched an opium lamp into the stove, sending a stream of blazing oil along the floor and setting the tinder-dry woodwork on fire. Within seconds the hall was ablaze and smoke mixed with the rancid odour of opium filled the narrow passageway.

As the detectives forced their way into the smoking den, the door to the room clanged shut behind them, trapping Ricci and Sinclair and seven hysterical addicts. One of the den's clients was still feeding fresh oil onto the flames.

opposite:
Foncie photo of Joe Ricci ca. 1940s.
PHOTO COURTESY LOUISE RICCI

below:
Gambling in Chinatown.
VANCOUVER PUBLIC LIBRARY #41613A

The only escape was from a window barred with iron rods set 50 feet above the ground. Realizing they couldn't break through the window grill, Ricci and Sinclair took turns attacking the window frame with the axe until the frame yielded.

Detective Inspectors John Jackson and John Jewitt had stationed themselves outside the ground floor exits. Jackson sent for backup, and was becoming increasingly worried as smoke poured from the burning building and windows burst from the heat.

Ricci, cut by glass from the breaking window and bleeding from an ugly gash to his right forearm, jumped first, spraining his ankle. Sinclair followed, injuring his knee in the fall.

Inspectors Jackson and Jewitt had ripped off their overcoats and were using them to break the fall of the Chinese addicts. One of the men fell on his back and was badly hurt, but the rest escaped the fire unharmed and were taken into custody.

Ricci had even managed to grab some of the evidence on the way through the burning room.

It was March 3, 1916.

braw:
Scottish term
meaning good, fine

Later, Sinclair told a reporter in his Scottish burr: "It does not sound much in the telling, but when you were there you were bound to do some braw figuring and I don't think we were ever in a tighter box."

VANCOUVER POLICE DEPARTMENT

"Besides being the most unobtrusive, the detective or 'plainclothes' man finds his work perhaps the most thankless of all. He may not share the publicity and glory of his valor or shrewdness because the exploiting of his personality damages his value as a secret agent of the department. His movements must be unheralded and his identity remains unrevealed if he is to be effective."
—Chief Constable James Anderson, City of Vancouver Police Department, 1921

The chief sure wasn't talking about Ricci and Sinclair.

Hardly low-profile police officers, Ricci and Sinclair were regularly front page news, and quickly became legendary up and down the Pacific Coast.

Ricci joined the department in 1912 and proved to be a natural at police work. He went from probationer to acting detective on the anti-gambling and Chinatown drug squad in less than a year. Donald Sinclair couldn't be more different. At six feet tall, the older man had four inches on Ricci. He'd joined the police force after six years with the Galashiels Borough Police in his native Scotland, made detective in 1914, and shortly after was partnered up with Ricci.

They were the odd couple right from the get-go. Ricci dressed with a Latin flare, often sporting a pinstripe suit and silk tie with a jade pin gleaming from the knot, topped off with a dapper black Borselino hat tilted at a jaunty angle. Sinclair, on the other hand, looked like he'd slept in his clothes.

They bickered constantly, yet they had the best arrest record in the department. In one year alone they arrested 150 drug addicts and peddlers. They knew every hideout, alley and underworld haunt in the East End, and were undaunted by the buildings in Chinatown with their electronically locking doors, twisting passageways, and hidden trapdoors.

blind pig:
establishments that
sold illegal booze

The duo regularly captured robbers and murderers, conducted hundreds of raids on opium dens, gambling joints, bootleggers, brothels and blind pigs, and seized hundreds of thousands of dollars worth of illegal drugs.

In 1919, the detectives were chasing Joseph Orchard Ebanka, a suspected burglar. After firing a warning shot and shouting for him to stop, Ricci fired from 50 feet, shooting the fleeing felon through both thighs. Rather than being severely disciplined, Ricci was commended on his excellent marksmanship.

In those days police didn't have to worry too much about legal niceties such as warrants, but would regularly break down locked doors with axes and crowbars, fists swinging, shooting first and asking questions later.

Joe Ricci (middle) and members of the Vancouver Police Department, ca. 1925. PHOTO COURTESY LOUISE RICCI

JOE RICCI (1889-1966)
2667 East Pender Street

Giuseppe (Joe) Ricci was born in Falvaterra, Italy in 1889. He worked in construction in the States, moved to Prince Rupert in 1906 and worked on the Grand Trunk Railway before becoming a foreman for the City of Vancouver. One night, in 1912 he had his coat stolen from his East Pender Street home. After badgering the desk sergeant about his stolen property, he was told they were doing the best that they

could. If Ricci thought he could do better he should join the police force.

As it happened, the Vancouver Police Department was struggling to clean up crime in the close-knit Italian community. When Ricci applied some weeks later, his understanding of English and Italian, along with an aggressive nature and an intimate knowledge of the bootleggers, pimps, and petty criminals in the city's Little Italy, qualified him for the job.

Ricci married Mary Rose Delong in April 1913. In 1922, he bought a lot at Slocan and East Pender and built his house, a simple structure with stone shipped over from Gibsons on the Sunshine Coast. The couple didn't have children, and Mary Rose died from cancer in 1929 at 40 years of age. Two years later, Ricci literally married the girl next door—Germaine Paquette, a 26-year-old

French Canadian who lived with her aunt. Germaine and her aunt, says Ricci's daughter Louise, were talented seamstresses.

Louise still lives in the house her father built. The house has been well maintained and looks much the same as it would have 90 years ago. Louise, who was born in 1932, grew up on her father's stories, and she has kept file boxes full of yellowed newspaper clippings of his exploits, as well as dozens of faded family photographs.

On the top of one of the boxes is a copy of Montreal's *Standard Newspaper* and an article about Ricci's involvement in the "Angry Tong Wars."

"Ricci's squad had been knocking off Chinatown's gambling dens so often and so successfully that the rival tongs soon were bitterly accusing each other of 'squealing' to police. They got madder and madder at each other at every raid, and soon took to jeering and threatening each other from doorways and street corners," wrote the reporter. "Finally the pent-up violence broke into a riot. Ricci dashed down with his squad and ran into a mass of yelling, biting, scratching Orientals in the middle of Pender Street East."

Ricci goes on to tell the reporter that it was a "real free-for-all."

"That's the first time I actually saw blood flow on the streets," he said. "We just collared the angry little fellows as fast as we could and loaded them in joy wagons. That took the starch out of them and they scattered."

Louise walks through her kitchen and onto the back porch. It was here, she says, during those Tong Wars of the 1920s that Chinese gangsters broke in to her father's house and threw chicken blood all over the cupboards as a warning for Ricci to stay away.

He did what he always did with threats, she said. He ignored them.

THE MURDER OF MALCOLM MACLENNAN

Louise says that the closest her father came to death was on the night of March 20, 1917, when Police Chief Malcolm MacLennan was killed in an East End shoot-out.

Robert Tait, 32, a drug addict, police informant and pimp from Detroit lived in an apartment over a grocery store at 522 East Georgia with his girlfriend, a prostitute named Frankie Russell.

Frankie Russell, 28, went under the aliases of Edith Rice and Annie Harrington. She had numerous arrests for prostitution, theft and drug possession. At one point she worked out of Maria Gomez's House of all Nations, a high-profile brothel on Alexander Street. She later became notorious in the press as the "white girl of the underworld."

After months went by in unpaid rent, the owner of the apartment block, Frank Smith, decided to evict Tait and Russell. When Smith entered the kitchen, he was greeted by Tait brandishing a shotgun. Tait told Smith, "leave or I'll blow your brains out." Smith left and called the police.

It was dark and raining by the time Detective John Cameron and three constables arrived and knocked on the kitchen door. Moments later a blast from the shotgun fired through the frosted glass of the door, catching Cameron in the face and tearing out one of his eyes. The other policemen, all of them cut and bleeding from shards of flying glass, grabbed Cameron and retreated back out into the street.

As Tait blasted away through the door, trying to kill as many police officers as he could, George Robb, 9, was walking from his house at 548 East Georgia to buy candy at the nearby store. The boy was killed by a bullet to his back from Tait's rifle.

Police sent for backup, and Deputy Chief Bill McRae, Inspectors John Jackson and George McLaughlin, Chief Malcolm MacLennan and detectives Ricci and Sinclair rushed to the scene.

above: Popular Chief Constable Malcolm MacLennan was murdered in a shoot-out with a drug dealer in 1917.
VANCOUVER POLICE MUSEUM #P00923

left: 522 East Georgia.
EVE LAZARUS PHOTO

15

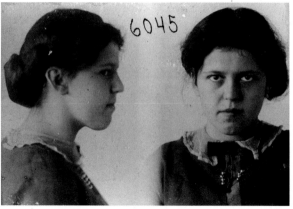

left: Robert Tait #P02002
right: Frankie Russell mug shot.
VANCOUVER POLICE MUSEUM

In a 1961 interview with the *Times Colonist*, Ricci told the reporter that police were in the hallway and Tait was in the kitchen with a loaded shotgun. Tait yelled out that he would use it if they came closer.

"The chief said he was going in to get Tait. I tried to reason with him because I was sure Tait would shoot. As soon as the chief stepped out of the hallway into the kitchen he got the full shotgun charge in the face, killing him on the spot," Ricci told the reporter. "I crept up as close to the doorway of the kitchen as I could and grabbed the dead chief by the ankle. I dragged him along the hallway out of range. Then we carried him out of the house to a police car.

"I still feel sick at my stomach when I think how close I came to getting the shotgun blast myself."

Four hours had passed since police had first entered the apartment, and when the gun battle ceased and police finally thought it was safe to reenter, they found that Tait had blown off the top of his head with a shotgun, fired by pulling the trigger with his toe. He was lying on top of Russell, who was unhurt, but heavily splattered with Tait's blood and a portion of his brain and skull. The walls were riddled with bullet holes, and police found two heavy calibre rifles, a double-barrelled shot gun, two revolvers, and a stockpile of ammunition.

Malcolm MacLennan, 44, was a popular chief who had served on the force for 20 years. He left a wife and two boys, aged 9 and 11, in the family home at 739 East Broadway. Frankie Russell was initially charged as an accomplice in the murders but was later acquitted. Detective John Cameron survived, and was named chief of police in 1933.

> "Mayor Gale, chairman of the police commission, has often remarked in discussions that the 'dry squad' officer's duties made him 'as popular as a skunk at a garden party.'"
> City of Vancouver Police Department, 1921.

THE DRY SQUAD

Following their success on the Drug Squad, in 1917 Ricci and Sinclair joined the Dry Squad.

When Prohibition was enforced in October 1917, bootlegging evolved from a cottage industry for enterprising East End families to a business for major operators who ran stills, blind pigs and bottle clubs.

Ricci and Sinclair proved just as effective capturing illicit stills and moonshine as they had breaking down the doors of opium dens.

The detectives turned up stills hidden away in attics and cellars and in barns and outhouses in the woods surrounding Vancouver, and they found thousands of gallons of mash, composed of everything from parsnips and turnips to grape seeds. The stills ranged from small producers to stills that could turn out 50 gallons a day.

Detective Joe Ricci, James Thorburn, deputy-collector, Inland Revenue Department and Detective Donald Sinclair with captured liquor stills, ca. 1918.
PHOTO COURTESY LOUISE RICCI.

During their time on the Dry Squad, the detectives arrested 36 men and collected $15,500 in fines.

In the Vancouver Police Department's 1917 report, Chief Constable McRae said that there had been a 65 percent decrease in drunkenness under the new Prohibition laws. "It is repeatedly remarked by the citizens what a pleasure it is to walk the downtown streets since the saloons were abolished," he wrote.

Will Woods has extensively researched Vancouver's Prohibition past for his Forbidden Vancouver tours. Booze was never completely illegal, he says. The British Columbia Prohibition Act allowed for "near-beer" bars that could sell liquor at a maximum concentration of 2.5 percent alcohol by volume. Before Prohibition, Vancouver was packed with saloons—roughly one for every 300 people. In Vancouver's early years, saloons opened all hours and served up whatever drinks they wanted at whatever price they liked.

Woods says that to circumvent Prohibition laws and avoid closing, many of these saloons reinvented themselves as near-beer bars, adding secret rooms out the back or in the basement where you could get a real drink.

"Records exist of crafty bar owners keeping bootleg beer and whisky in pitchers next to a bathtub full of water," he says. "In a police raid, the owners would dump the liquor into the bath and bring the alcohol content below 2.5 percent, avoiding prosecution."

Blind pigs—typically rundown illegal drinking and gambling dens run by organized crime—sprung up all over the city and specialized in the sale of moonshine.

"Blind pigs existed in warehouses, basements, private homes, even on board boats in False Creek and Burrard Inlet," says Woods. "Take a walk down Gastown's Blood Alley today and you can well imagine ducking into a blind pig."

Prohibition was a cash cow for the government. Fines received by the city treasury averaged between $10,000 and $12,000 a month, and seizures and forfeitures of booze ran to well over half a million dollars in value.

DRUG TRADE

More serious than citizens making and drinking illegal booze was the drug trade, which was growing in size and organization.

By 1919, the Dry Squad had increased in size and duties were split evenly between eradicating Vancouver of booze and the "drug evil." In a story of that year that is eerily similar to some of today's headlines, US officials called Vancouver the drug distribution centre responsible for the vast majority of their country's narcotics. Shortly afterwards, Ricci and Sinclair made what was then the largest drug seizure in the Western Hemisphere.

At the 3 East Broadway premises of J.J. Wing, the two detectives discovered a staggering supply of drugs packed into a trunk and hidden beneath the floor of a room in the house. Along with the drugs, the detectives also found letters from all over the US which showed that an organized trafficking ring existed.

The discovery of the trafficking ring coincided with a sharp increase in the use of drugs in Vancouver and other cities in Canada. Ricci and Sinclair threw themselves into their work, raiding dozens of addresses in Chinatown and the East End.

One of their biggest successes was a huge bust at 73 East Pender Street in 1920. When the detectives entered the apartment of Chow King Poe they found a small compartment hidden over the stairway. Behind a pair of sliding doors they found piles of old clothes, tin cans, and broken toys. Sinclair tapped the floor and heard a hollow sound. He lifted one of the planks. Hidden amongst the rubbish, he found opium, cocaine, heroin, and morphine with a street value in the hundreds of thousands of dollars.

During their two years of operations, Ricci and Sinclair seized close to $500,000 of illegal drugs.

THE BLACK HAND

Today's Italian crime syndicates are known as the Mafia or the Cosa Nostra, but in the 1920s, the term "Black Hand" (*La Mano Nera*) described an Italian extortion racket that was well established in major Italian communities throughout North America. Typically, a member of the Black Hand Society would send a letter to a target threatening violence, kidnapping, arson or even murder if they didn't pay protection money. The letter was often decorated with a smoking gun, a noose, a knife dripping with blood or piercing a human heart, and accompanied with the message: "held up in the universal gesture of warning" scrawled in thick black ink.

In November 1923, Ricci was going through the circulars and pictures of wanted criminals, when he stopped at one, sat back, and whistled softly. Starring back at him was the face of Dominic Delfino, a lieutenant and hit man for the Black Hand Society who was wanted by every police department in the US after his spectacular escape from jail several years before. Just a few hours earlier, one of Ricci's Italian informants had tipped him off that a "very bad Italian—maybe a murderer" was being held in a Nelson jail on an immigration charge. The prisoner, Ricci's informer told him, had boasted: "I shot my way out of the death house, and they'll never hold me very long."

Ricci familiarized himself with the details of the case. Delfino had been held in a Lakawanna county jail in Pennsylvania and charged with multiple murders. Before he could be transferred to his execution in New York, two of his colleagues, disguised as nuns, managed to smuggle in a saw and a revolver. Delfino escaped, murdering four guards on the way out.

Ricci decided to play a hunch and went to Nelson to see for himself. Delfino wouldn't talk, but the detective identified him from the mug shot. Delfino was sent back to the States and died in the electric chair. Ricci received front page headlines and collected a $500 reward.

Around the same time that Ricci was being lauded as a hero for his capture of the notorious Delfino, he was contacted by Frank Rosso, a 36-year-old Italian who ran a grocery and tobacconist store at 121 Lonsdale Avenue in North Vancouver. Rosso told Ricci that he'd received demands for money from the Black Hand Society, and had been threatened with death if he didn't pay up. Ricci investigated, but Rosso became frightened and refused to proceed because of his fear of the Society.

Less than two years later, Rosso was found butchered in his home at the back of the Lonsdale Avenue store. Because he was found hacked to death with an axe—just like one of the threats in the letters that he'd received—police initially believed it was the work of the Black Hand. Ricci was called back from holidays to help with the investigation. After learning that Rosso didn't trust banks and often kept up to $1,000 in cash at his shop, the police investigation ruled out the Black Hand and turned to robbery. Blood hounds tracked the killer's scent to the waterfront and a few days later, Charles Henry White, known in the underworld as "Sonny," was arrested for Rosso's brutal murder. He had made his getaway from North Vancouver in a canoe.

"I've had a bellyful of police work and criminals," Ricci *(right)* told a reporter after he left the force. "The crooks are too dumb today to make it worthwhile."
PHOTO CA. 1950 COURTESY LOUISE RICCI

CORRUPTION IN THE FORCE

In 1926, Ricci was assigned to the Morality Squad. Sinclair refused to go and even threatened to resign. It was the end of the odd couple.

Ricci, said Inspector John Jackson, complained bitterly at the transfer. "He did not like to be separated from Sinclair, and Sinclair was one who would not work on women, in prostitution." Ricci, said Jackson, got "pretty fair results." But his career, and that of Donald Sinclair's, would never be the same.

As Ricci told the Lennie Commission into police corruption two years later, he found that there was a lack of commitment from senior officers to stamp out vice, gambling or blind pigs.

"It was an understood thing that no women be arrested every other day and every other night, but to bring them in once or twice a month," he said. Gambling, he said was so "wide open" that it was a disgrace to the uniformed men and the police force.

Ricci and Sinclair were two of 98 witnesses who gave evidence. Ricci testified that when he wanted to close down brothels he was told by a superior that it was

understood between Mayor L.D. Taylor and Attorney General Manson that a certain number of disorderly houses had to run on both the East and the West sides.

When Commissioner Lennie asked Ricci why he didn't raid Joe Celona's brothels, Ricci answered: "Do you want me to lose my job? If the bosses see fit to let them run, that is up to them."

The Lennie Commission shook up the police force. Chief Henry Long and Detective Inspector George McLaughlin were fired. Mayor Taylor was never convicted of anything, but the smell of corruption clung to him and he lost the election to William Malkin later that year. Sinclair came out relatively unscathed, but Ricci was one of eight detectives who lost their jobs when the police force was restructured under the newly appointed Chief W.J. Bingham.

In 1929 and on the eve of the Depression, Ricci became the manager of the beer parlour at the Royal Hotel on Granville Street. Louise Ricci says her father told her that—after 16 years as Vancouver's most heralded crime fighter—he was lucky to come out alive.

Sinclair remained for a few more years and retired in 1935. He died from heart failure two years later at age 55 in his home on Woodland Drive.

THE WEST COAST CENTRAL CLUB

In 1948, Ricci founded the West Coast Central Club right next to the police station and courts on Main Street. Louise Ricci and her sister Rosemary worked at the club, Louise eventually taking over as manager when her father had a stroke seven years later. While the club appealed to fisherman, longshoremen, and loggers, it also attracted Ricci's former police colleagues—and the people who kept them in business—judges, bad guys, and newspaper reporters like Jack Wasserman and Jack Webster.

"Jack Webster used to sit beside the planters so nobody would see him," says Louise. "I'd serve him screwdrivers."

She remembers Officer Bernie "Whistling" Smith—who earned his nickname for whistling while he patrolled the streets—coming into the club, as well as crime boss Joe Celona and his ex-wife Josie; the Honorable Dolores Holmes, daughter of BC Supreme Court Judge Angelo Branca; and Judge Les Bewley.

"I used to put the judges in a room at the front, we called it the private dining room, and they'd have cocktails and talk shop," she says.

Soon after Ricci opened his club, he rejoined the police force as a court interpreter. He told a newspaper reporter at the time that he no longer had any interest in chasing bad guys.

"I've had a bellyful of police work and criminals," he said. "The crooks are too dumb today to make it worthwhile."

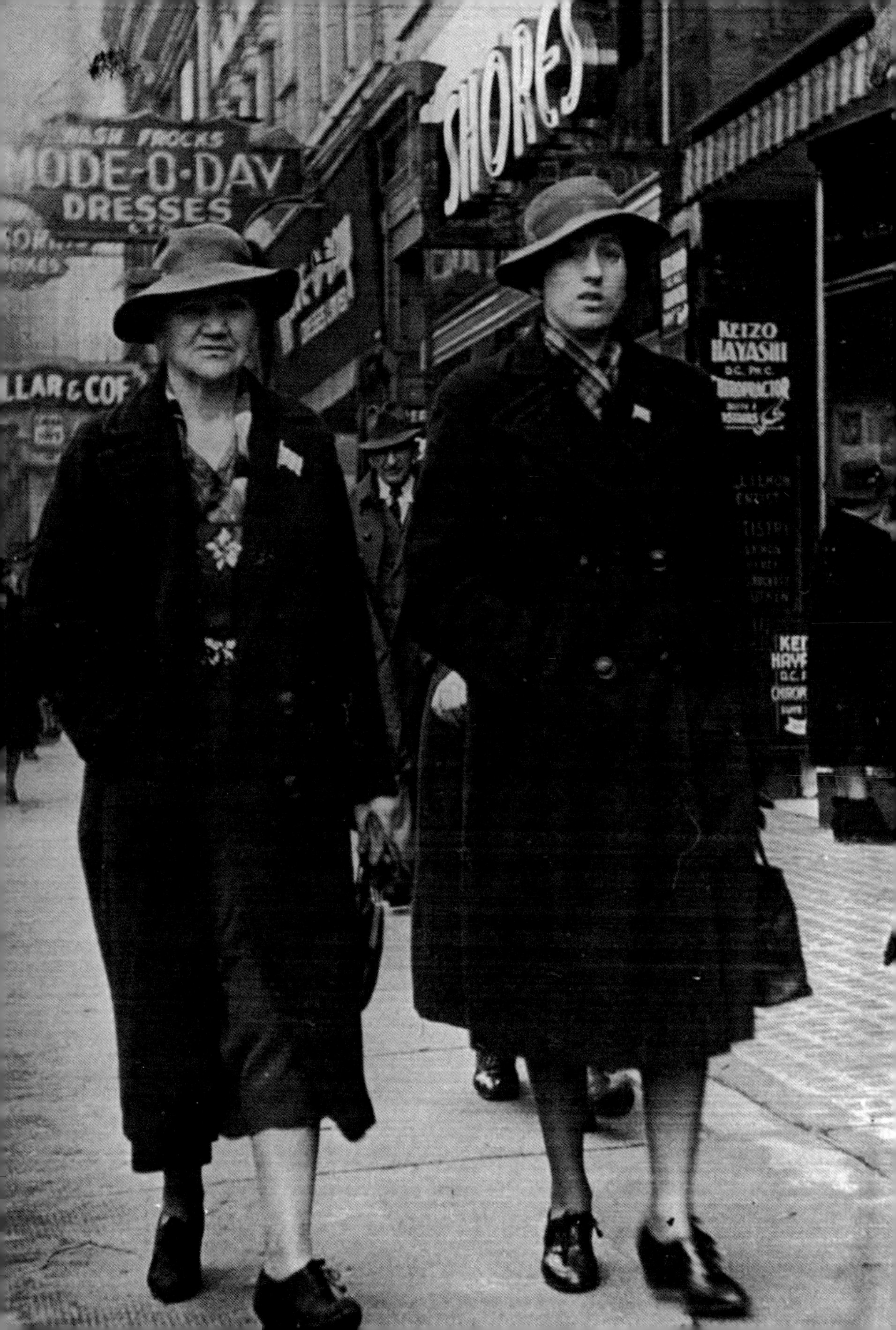
FROCKS
MODE-O-DAY
DRESSES
SHORES
KEIZO
HAYASHI

CHAPTER 2

Lurancy Harris's Beat

"The Policewoman should be of a sensible temperament but have a sense of humour. She should be diplomatic, mature, well-disciplined, and resourceful. She must have an infinite amount of patience, but not easily shocked or disturbed, be able to meet all levels of people, and be able to control her feelings and emotions. Her manner must be pleasant and agreeable but firm and, when necessary, commanding without being overbearing. She should be of above average intelligence and have high moral standards."
From an undated Vancouver Police Department report.

Lurancy Durkee Harris, otherwise known as Lou, moved to Vancouver from Yarmouth, Nova Scotia in 1911. She rented a small apartment on Robson at Howe, where the Chapters-Indigo store is today, and set herself up as a dressmaker in Vancouver's booming pre-war economy. One day in 1912—the same year Joe Ricci joined the force—Harris was flipping through a newspaper when an ad caught her eye. The Vancouver Police Department was looking for "two good reliable women" to form the nucleus of a women's protective division centred around issues of morality and protecting the safety of wayward women and children. The job sounded a lot more adventurous and stable than sewing. At the age of 48, Harris was hired by the VPD, along with Minnie Eakin Millar, a 34-year-old nurse from Ireland. The two became the first women police officers in Canada.

Foncie photo of two police officers, 400 block West Hastings. ca. 1940s.
VANCOUVER POLICE MUSEUM #P03213

OFFICERS HARRIS AND MILLAR
Harris and Millar were sworn in as fourth class constables on June 17, 1912, the lowest rank in the department, with a salary of $80 a month. The women were given full police powers—everything except the right to carry a gun or wear a uniform. It would be another 35 years until women wore police uniforms, and six decades before women had the right to carry firearms and were assigned to regular patrol duties like their male counterparts.

Especially in the early days, Harris and Millar had to make do with long heavy skirts, button-up jackets, hats, gloves and purses to carry valuables.

Harris made her first arrest five months after she was hired. Her name is in the prison record books for arresting 38-year-old Annie Smith #5705, alias Mrs. Stanfield, a bigamist from England. Annie told police that she believed that her husband, Mr. Smith, was dead. She had answered a personal ad in a Spokane newspaper and, through the ad, met and married Mr. Stanfield in 1909. Under grounds of cruelty, she divorced Stanfield and fled to Vancouver with her two small children. Stanfield somehow unearthed Smith, and the two men went to police in Vancouver. Annie was found "technically guilty," but given a suspended sentence according to an entry in the prison record book "on account of the troubles and suffering she had endured."

Lurancy Harris ca. 1915.
CVA A-30-83

They were given no training and told to focus their work on low-income and poorly educated women and girls. The thought at the time was that any woman, even those with money and some influence, were vulnerable to "inappropriate and unfeminine" behaviour.

Harris and Millar patrolled dance halls, cabarets, pool halls, beer parlours, parks, and beaches—anywhere that young women might get themselves into trouble. They also acted as matrons in the jail and escorted female victims and suspects to their court appearances. The two constables could also make arrests.

Much of their work revolved around "white slavery" and "the social evil"—the emotional terms used at the time to describe prostitution.

Harris and Millar had their hands full. As the economy weakened and as women were laid off from low-status jobs, prostitution became a growth industry in Vancouver, one that attracted local girls as well as Americans and runaways from all over the country.

As J.W. Wilkinson wrote in the *British Columbia Federationist* of 1912: "Supposing I were a girl, good-looking, young and full of the joy of life, and I found that by working in a department store I could get only from $4 to $10 a week, and that by obliging my outwardly virtuous men friends from time to time I could make from $50 to $200 a week, which should I be likely to do?"

Sending prostitutes and madams to jail was actively discouraged, as Harris found when she escorted 14 convicted prostitutes to Oakalla prison.

"I took a load over there and they turned them all loose. They were not welcome at all," she said years later. "It was shortly after I joined the department and I was left like a bump on a log and didn't know what to do. I took all these prisoners over and landed there and they were turned loose."

Attorney General William Bowser was publicly against jailing prostitutes. Instead he came up with the idea to round up the women, take them to court and sentence them to six months in jail. He then had them released and told to come back a week later to begin serving their time. Most headed back to the United States, where they had originated, temporarily solving the prostitution problem in Vancouver.

Bowser, who had defended madams before becoming Attorney General, said the jail didn't have room for these women, and besides he felt that reform rather than punishment was far more effective. "I want to know what good it would do to put these women in jail for six months. Has anything been accomplished when they get out?" he said. "If anything, I think they are more vicious against society."

His attitude wasn't exactly benevolent or particularly enlightened. Bowser told reporters that prostitutes were "mentally lacking."

Lurancy Harris built this house in 1916 and planted the monkey tree.
EVE LAZARUS PHOTO

LURANCY HARRIS (1864–1947)
1836 Venables Street

Six months after she was hired, Lurancy Harris got the first big break in her career in the form of Lorena Mathews. In 1908, Mathews made headlines from Oklahoma to Edmonton when she bolted across the continent with her two children and Jim Chapman, her 25-year-old black lover who was suspected of helping her murder her much older husband.

The case was one of the most sensational in Oklahoma history, and daily reading for Canadians. Lorena Mathews bought a ranch for Chapman to run outside of Edmonton, and opened up a boarding house in the city. Rumours circulated that it was a brothel. Two years later, police from Stillwater, Oklahoma received a tip that the couple was living in Edmonton, and began extradition proceedings. Chapman was returned and tried and convicted for murder. Mathews fought the charges for the next two years. When it looked like she would lose, she grabbed the kids and boarded a train to Vancouver where she was promptly arrested.

Officer Harris was assigned to accompany Mathews back to Oklahoma to stand trial—a train trip of over 2,500 kilometres. Their first stop was Seattle, and Harris handcuffed her unhappy prisoner and deposited her at the city jail before checking herself into the local YWCA. The next day they continued on to Denver and Harris again took Mathews along to the local jail to spend the night. When the women reached Guthrie, Oklahoma, Harris turned her prisoner over to the authorities, spent the night, and returned home the next day.

Mathews was eventually acquitted of the murder.

Harris was listed as Mrs. Lawrence D. Harris in the city directories right up until 1920. No such person existed. She was briefly married to John Henry Harris, a doctor back in Yarmouth, and it's unclear why she didn't use his name, but it was likely a marriage of convenience.

After Dr. Harris's wife Evaline died in the early 1890s, Dr. Harris, then 51, married one of his servants—Hannah May Porter, 31, in 1895. Hannah died two years later while giving birth to their daughter, Lucille May Harris. The following year, Dr. Harris married Lurancy Durkee, then 34. He died in 1902, and Lurancy Harris became a widow.

Lucille, who became known just as May, moved to St. Catherines, Ontario to live with her aunt, and a few years later, Harris moved out west.

In 1916, Harris purchased a lot on Venables Street, planted a monkey tree, and paid $1,500 to have a small craftsman house built on the property. Some years later, Sergeant William Kuncr, 13 years her junior, moved into the house with her.

By all accounts Lurancy Harris had an amazing career. In 1924 she was promoted to inspector, although she was kept at the pay scale of a sergeant. She retired five years later, aged 65.

Wayne Harris was born in 1945, and that year he and his mother and father moved into the house next door to Lurancy Harris and Kuner. Wayne has no recollection of his great aunt Lurancy, but remembers Kuner very well.

"I got the impression Mr. Kuner was like a father to my dad," he says. "He was a big guy with a moustache and my dad was always faithfully visiting him when he could."

Harris lived until age 84. Her handwritten will witnessed by Eva Pelton, shows that she left $100 to Wayne's grandmother—Lou Wealthy Harris who had moved out from Yarmouth to take care of her towards the end of her life—and an aquamarine ring with small diamonds, her wedding ring and gold chain with heart-shaped slip to her stepdaughter May Harris. She left her house and belongings to her "friend", William Kuner until his death, and then directed that the house should be sold and anything remaining divided between two children's charities.

above:
Officer Harris escorted Lorena Mathews back to Oklahoma to stand trial for murder.
PHOTO OF LORENA MATHEWS IN 1913 COURTESY OF RESEARCH DIVISION OF THE OKLAHOMA HISTORICAL SOCIETY #19383.10

right:
Wenonah Apartments and home of Minnie Millar.
EVE LAZARUS PHOTO

Wayne Harris visited Kuner in the house in 1966 shortly before the older man's death. Kuner, he said, had a profound influence on his choosing a career with the RCMP.

"Their home was beautiful," he said. "It had a gas fireplace, solid wood throughout and Mr. Kuner always gave my brother and me a coin as we left. I always insisted on petting the mounted deer head as we left. My dad lifted me up so I could do so."

Mark Lindsay, a carpenter, bought the house in 1983. He did a huge renovation 15 years later and added a second floor.

The monkey tree is still there, towering over the house.

MINNIE MILLAR (1878–1927)
2703 Main Street

Minnie Millar arrived in Vancouver in 1909 and worked as a nurse. Shortly after she was hired by the Vancouver Police Department, she moved in with Lurancy Harris at her apartment at 111 East Broadway.

Millar had one moment of notoriety: in August 1912 she became front page news in both daily papers for notching up the first official arrest by a female officer in Canada. According to newspaper accounts, Constable

Millar was disguised as a "dainty damsel" and sent to English Bay to catch William S. Borden. Borden was described as a "big husky individual" who apparently liked to "make himself obnoxious to women on the beach."

Borden was charged with indecent conduct towards women. "It is alleged that Borden spied her on the sands and that she instantly captured his heart and person, returning the former but lodging the latter in the cells at police headquarters," wrote the reporter.

Millar, who remained single all her life, left after a short time on the job and returned to nursing, moving into the Wenonah Apartments at Main and East 11th. There is no explanation for why she left—though discrimination and sexism on the job must have been intense, and working conditions dismal. The women's appointment to the police department had come about because of pressure from local mission and church groups, not from inside the force, and it's probably not much of a stretch to suggest that they were resented by their male colleagues.

Yet, in 1919, Millar was back at the police force, and in 1920 she was one of three female constables working under Harris in the Women's Division. The other two constables to join the squad that year were Evelyn LeSueur and Eva Pelton.

Millar died from a stroke in 1927. Her death certificate listed "police officer" as her occupation.

EVA ST. CLAIRE PELTON (1873–1950)
Banff Apartments – 1201 Georgia Street

Born in Nova Scotia, Eva Pelton moved out to Vancouver with her mother, Mrs. Sanford Pelton, and two brothers. Guy was a business manager, and Gerald a barrister and solicitor. They lived at the Banff Apartments on the corner of Georgia and Bute Street. In 1927, she and Guy moved to the Rougemont Apartments at Robson and Bidwell where she lived until her retirement from the Vancouver Police Department in 1930.

EVELYN DAISY LESUEUR (1881–1959)
7828 Prince Albert

A former bookkeeper at Beaver Interurban Auto Transfer, Evelyn LeSueur was 38 when she joined the force in 1919. Two years later she was officially fired for "incompetence" and for being "unfit for the duties of constable." Unofficially, LeSueur was a well-educated, intelligent, firebrand who had strong feminist views and unconventional religious beliefs.

MRS. PELTON

top: Minnie Millar was the first woman constable to make an arrest in Canada in 1912. PHOTO COURTESY VANCOUVER POLICE MUSEUM #P06565

above: Eva St. Clair Pelton, ca. 1928. PHOTO COURTESY VANCOUVER POLICE MUSEUM

As an early and active member of the Pioneer Political Equality League, LeSueur gave lectures on how the law affected women. At one of the meetings that LeSueur attended, the police chief came under criticism for his decision to appoint a male to a judicial role. Even though LeSueur did not participate in the heated discussion, the police chief learned of her presence and demanded her resignation for what he told her was her "openly expressed disloyalty and ridicule of myself and the police department."

The feisty LeSueur refused and appealed the decision to the board of police commissioners. Following a lengthy hearing, the board made no decision and the chief and LeSueur were told to try and settle their differences and come back to the next meeting. Fortunately for the disgruntled chief, fate intervened.

A week after the board's indecision, LeSueur was at a dinner party where the Reverend Macaulay was a guest. When he asked her what her religious views were she told him that she was born a Methodist, but no longer belonged to any particular church. While she believed in God, she told him, she didn't believe that Jesus was his son, just that he was a good man. The outraged Reverend wrote to the police board, saying that LeSueur was not fit to look after young girls. She was fired.

LeSueur subsequently became a probation officer with the Juvenile Court and Detention Home, where she worked until her retirement.

Not wanting to hire another feminist, the police department played it safe for the next two decades by hiring mostly policemen's widows and keeping them busy with inside duties.

PHYLLIS MORTIMORE (1917–2009)
Rougemont Apartments - 1689 Robson Street

When Phyllis Mortimore joined the force in 1943, she reported to the second floor of the Cordova Street Police Station, opposite the prosecutor's office and just a short distance from the jail elevator and court rooms. Her starting salary was $106, not much of a bump up from Harris's and Millar's $80 wage three decades before. At that time, the Women's Division still focused on child neglect and family problems and employed five women. Four of the women, including the department head, were widows of former police officers and their duties were limited mostly to escorting female prisoners to jail and to court, supervising parolees, and assisting detectives when required.

"When I first came on the force we made calls on foot or took a streetcar," says Phyllis Mortimore.
PHOTO CA. 1950 COURTESY VANCOUVER POLICE MUSEUM #P02421

When Mortimore was sworn in to the force, a police inspector told her and a fellow woman recruit: "Now girls, I'm going to tell you something," she recalled to a *Vancouver Sun* reporter in 1987. "If you want to keep the respect of the men, don't get familiar with them, don't call them by their first names."

Mortimore was already well acquainted with the Women's Division through her mother Edna, who was a member of the Local Council of Women and had worked closely with Lurancy Harris, Eva Pelton and Evelyn

28

LeSueur during their tenure with the force. Edna Mortimore won a Citizen of the Year Award in 1945 for volunteer work with pensioners and fighting for women's rights.

Mortimore's father built the Rougemont Apartment building at Robson and Bidwell in 1911, and she knew Pelton and her brother Guy when they moved there in 1927.

Pelton and Harris had left the police force by the start of the Depression, and Mortimore reports that the Women's Division was almost disbanded as a cost cutting measure. When Harris died in 1947, Mortimore represented the police force at her funeral. She did the same three years later, when Pelton passed away.

Although policewomen were still four years away from wearing a regulation police uniform, the women wore an unofficial uniform of a white shirt, navy skirt and jacket.

"When I first came on the force we made calls on foot or took a street car and it was in 1948 that we were first permitted to drive the police cars ourselves on calls," said Mortimore. "There was a team of detectives who drove the escort car with female prisoners to Oakalla Prison Farm in company of a policewoman."

APPROACHING PARITY

Mortimore never married, but if she had she would have had to leave the force, and in those early days, if a woman married a fellow officer, he was demoted.

Forty years after the first policewoman was hired, women became eligible for training. They could learn to shoot, and even though Mortimore became an ace shot and a member of a pistol club, women were not permitted to carry firearms on duty until 1973, the year before she retired.

In 1957 Mortimore was riding up in the elevator when she found herself alone with Police Chief George Archer. "I tackled him and said, 'How about getting equal pay for the women?' and he said, "What do the women do that's the same as the men?' I said, 'Everything,'" she told the *Vancouver Sun* reporter.

Archer had Mortimore write a report outlining the duties policewomen performed at the time to justify the pay increase. But as Mortimore soon found out, while women could compete for promotion, they wouldn't necessarily get the job.

That same year, Mortimore was one of 127 people to write the exam for promotion to corporal. Besides being the only woman to pass the exam, she received the top marks. Instead of promoting her, the horrified department reclassified the female constables as "policewomen," effectively stopping any promotion within the general ranks. Mortimore was eventually promoted inside the Women's Division to corporal, and in 1969 she made sergeant.

Nancy Hewitt, the inspector in charge of the Women's Division and the person most responsible for the gradual changes, died the same year Mortimore received her promotion, and unfortunately for Mortimore, women on the force took another backslide.

Once again, policewomen were taken off street duties and relegated to answering the phones and escorting female prisoners to court. Occasionally they were given a break from these duties when they were asked to go undercover as prostitutes for the vice squad.

By 1974, the year Mortimore retired, the force abandoned the Women's Division. The following year, Marilyn Simms became the first woman to make Detective.

CHAPTER 3

The Social Evil

L ike any port city with a constant flow of sailors, loggers, miners and fisherman, Vancouver had a well-established and mobile red light district. In those early days, brothels were not only tolerated, but were an important economic generator for the young city. Fines, ranging from $15 for the prostitutes to $50 for the keepers, shored up city coffers, while a high-class brothel might employ a cook and housekeepers, bartenders and musicians. The industry supported cab drivers and paid high rents to land owners. The girls, or "inmates" as they were known by police, needed regular health checkups, clothes and cosmetics.

In 1900, when the city had eight men for every woman, the red light district was firmly established on Dupont Street (now East Pender) and stayed there for several years. Pictures from the period show wagons on an unpaved road with two-storey wood framed buildings that housed a mix of residential and commercial businesses. By 1903, Mayor Thomas Neelands was calling for the closure of the brothels. Several Aldermen disagreed, wanting to confine "the social evil" to one district rather than spread the madams and the prostitutes all over the city.

The Aldermen won that round, but in the spring of 1904 police raided several houses and charged absentee landlord Dora Reno under the vagrancy bylaw. The crown alleged that Reno, who lived in a nice apartment in a better part of town, had illegally profited by her ownership of the brothel at 140 Dupont. Reno hired future Attorney General William Bowser, who argued that the city had no authority to pass the law and won the case. The madams stayed put for the next two years.

Then, in 1906, police responded to another outbreak of moral fervour, by clamping down on the red light district and forcing the prostitutes out of Dupont Street. As predicted, the prostitutes set up shop along Canton Alley and Shanghai Alley, and onto Harris Street (later renamed East Georgia.)

OFFICIALS ARE SHOCKED
"Conditions in Restricted District are Worst in City's History. Innocent youths invited into lowest dives. Officials are shocked," screamed a *Province* headline in

Joe Celona with his lawyer Angelo Branca at the 1955 police probe.
THE PROVINCE PHOTO 215316494

Prisoner record cards (handwritten):

Name _Alice Young_
Alias _Dead // England_
Nativity _England_
Occupation _Prostitute_
Criminal Occup. _Inmate - du..._
Date of Arrest _Sept..._
Where Arrested _Van..._
By Whom Arrested _Dets Kille..._
Crime Charged _Vagra..._
How Disposed of _with..._
Marks, Scars, etc. _3 vac marks_
6049
U 00.14
U 00

Alice was an inmate of ... Alexander Street. Her ... demanded her to leave ... fired several shots from ... with 6048

237
21 ...
13 R 00.12
17 R 00

Name _Archibald Young_
Alias
Nativity _Scotland_ Age _28_
Occupation _Laborer_ Height _5-6½_
Criminal Occup. _Shooting with intent_ Weight _142_
Date of Arrest _Sept 9th 1913_ Build _medium_
Where Arrested _Vancouver_ Complexion _Fresh_
By Whom Arrested _Dets Champion & Killeen_ Color of Eyes _Pale Blue_
Crime Charged _No Charges Laid_ Color of Hair _Dark Brown_
How Disposed of _Allowed to go [Dec 4th]_ Color of Moustache _none_
Marks, Scars, etc. _Left leg of below knee - Bullet wound on left ... Both hands ..._ Color of Beard _none_
Style of Beard _none_
6048
Dead //

Young requested his wife to leave a house of prostitution and on her refusing to do so, he began to shoot first at the inmates - then at the Police. He was finally shot through the Ankle himself & was taken to the Hospital where his left leg was amputated at the Calf. Brought from the hospital on Dec 4th 1913 - when the surveillance against Young was withdrawn on account of the Injuries he had received.

Archie Young, 28, was looking for his wife. Alice, a pretty 21-year-old girl with dark hair and blue eyes, had decided a brothel was preferable to life with the mean Scot she had married. When Archie tracked her down at Mabel Clark's brothel on Alexander Street, she refused to leave. He shot her with his revolver, and then turned his pale blue eyes on the other prostitutes and began to fire first at them, and then at detectives Champion and Killeen who had burst through the door. The detectives returned fire and shot him in both legs and in his left arm. Police took Young to hospital, where he had his left leg amputated and a bullet removed from his right leg. He was charged with "shooting with intent," but charges were dropped on his release from hospital seven weeks later "on account of the injuries he had received."

Prisoner Record Book,
September 9, 1913.

1906, after city officials took a reporter on a tour of the brothels one Saturday night.

The city councillors found a long string of red lights outside the doors of the brothels, some displaying glittering name signs with a crowd of men lined up outside. Scantily dressed women "attired in the briefest of skirts" beckoned to them as they passed from behind curtains and half-opened doors, inviting them to enter. "During the entire tour of the evening, not a policeman was in evidence," noted the reporter.

In fact, Police Chief Sam North had recently been fired when a madam testified in court that she paid him $150 so that she could run her Dupont Street business. North was replaced as VPD chief by Colin Chisholm, who favoured a central red light district and was clearly frustrated by the decision to kick the prostitutes out of Dupont Street without interference.

"Prostitutes were never scattered throughout the City to the extent they are at the present time and this I attribute to the demand being carried out, and to the zeal of certain misguided persons, in their anxiety to perform the impossible—Extermination of Prostitution," wrote Chief Chisholm in the Annual Report of 1906. "The crucifixion of the evil, could not even be accomplished by the Apostles, according to St. Paul, far less by a chief of police or any association, however good their intentions."

Aside from prostitution, it was a busy year for police, noted Chisholm. Police had taken 14 "insane to the Asylum," cited 15 people for "furious driving," another 15 "Hindus for begging" and returned six lost children and nine dogs to their owners.

ALEXANDER STREET

In 1912, Chief Rufus Chamberlin reluctantly clamped down again on prostitution and sent the madams scattering. The following year he optimistically wrote in his report under the heading "Social Evil": "336 arrests made of women of immoral character and a large number of convictions obtained for the illicit sale of liquor among this class. This evil while not at all eradicated is receiving the strict attention of the department. There is no restricted district in the City of Vancouver at this time."

Apparently no one had told Marie Gomez, Dolly Darlington, Alice Bernard, or a dozen or so other madams who had either renovated existing buildings or built luxurious and expensive brothels along Alexander Street that year.

In 1912, the overwhelming majority of brothels on Alexander Street were operated by women who employed women. In a world that offered few business opportunities, brothel keeping was an attractive proposition, one that easily covered fines and was worth the risk of jail. Prostitution also became a viable alternative for women who otherwise faced unemployment, under-employment, a life of drudgery in domestic service, low paying service jobs, or work in filthy factories.

opposite: COURTESY OF THE VANCOUVER POLICE MUSEUM

below: Alexander Street was the unofficial red light district in 1912. #514 was designed by Woolridge and McMullen architects. EVE LAZARUS PHOTO

bottom: 504 Alexander Street was designed as a brothel by William T. Whiteway, the same architect who designed the Holden Building and the Sun Tower. EVE LAZARUS PHOTO

Madams called themselves landladies or boarding-house keepers in the Census, and the prostitutes claimed legitimate occupations such as seamstresses, telephone operators, waitresses, nurses, housekeepers and milliners. Prisoner record books of the time show a diverse group of white, black, Indian and Asian women who came from all over Canada and the United States, citing religious beliefs ranging from Roman Catholic to free thinker.

Marie Gomez designed and built her house at 578 Alexander for $9,000, and it soon became known as the House of all Nations by police and patrons. Marie was so proud of her new building that she had her name spelled out in mosaic tiles in the front entrance.

Alice Bernard, who was born in France in 1873, hired architects Woolridge and McMullen to design and build a $14,500 two-storey brick rooming house that still stands at 514 Alexander. That same year, Alice paid $900 to have the architects transform a 1902 one-storey house at 620 Alexander into suitable brothel material.

Lucille Gray, who had previously worked for a madam named Cleo Devere on Harris Street, hired Wilson & Wilson architects to design an "apartment" building at 512 Alexander Street for $17,300.

Kathryn A. Maynard poured $15,000 into building a grand brick building at 504 Alexander Street, designed by William T. Whiteway, a respected architect who designed dozens of buildings, including the Holden Building on East Hastings and the Sun Tower. Maynard's building still stands.

Another surviving brothel building is one founded by Dolly Darlington. Located at 500 Alexander at the intersection of Jackson Street, it is still an imposing brick structure. Ironically,

the building became the headquarters for the British Seaman's Mission, and in 2013 sold to the Atira Women's Resource Society. Janice Abbott, CEO of Atira, says that part of the appeal of buying the 18-room building to house at-risk teenage girls, was because of its history as a brothel.

"Most of the young women who live here right now have been on the street since they were 12 or 13," she says. "Our goal is to get them using less and working less and [the building] is meant to be transitional so after about a year or two they should be going somewhere else."

top: Built as a brothel for Dolly Darlington in 1912, 500 Alexander Street became the headquarters for the British Seaman's Mission. Today it houses at-risk teenage girls. Curt Lang Photo, 1972. VPL 85872CC

above: 500 Alexander Street is now owned by the Atira Women's Resource Society. EVE LAZARUS PHOTO

The best of the brothels were classy affairs, tastefully designed to give the feeling of wealth and luxury. Expensive wallpaper adorned the walls, the parlours were equipped with fine furnishings, usually a piano, and a bar and bartender or Madam to dispense overpriced booze. And, of course, there were elaborately decked-out bedrooms. The girls were often well spoken, always beautifully dressed, and the brothels attracted a wealthy clientele.

SCANDALOUS

A writer for a short-lived scandal sheet called *The Truth* was sent on assignment in November 1912 to report on the brothels of Alexander Street after, as he noted in his article, his boss was arrested while enjoying Louise Brown's establishment.

"Louise weighs about a quarter of a ton, and certainly looks it," observed the reporter. "This is 516 Alexander Street, where the editor got pinched, and it certainly seems as if this dump is enjoying an era of prosperity."

Alice Bernard's brothel had the best dancing pavilion in Vancouver, with tunes played by a "sun burned lady" on the piano. The price of entry was a 25-cent glass of beer.

Alice's house, he said, "takes the cake."

"Alice herself is an elderly old damsel and certainly doesn't occupy a niche in the world's gallery of beautiful women. But what she can do in the way of juggling drinks at 25 cents a throw, would make many a younger woman turn green with envy."

The reporter was equally impressed with Marie Gomez's House of all Nations, and conveyed his impressions in the racist language of the day. "You can get everything there from a chocolate coloured damsel up to a Swede girl. They are mixed so thoroughly that you don't know whether you are in a coon joint or visiting a foreign city.

"We ran across some of the sweetest scented looking bunch of females we ever saw, and they were strewn all over the street in dazzling costumes of modern make," he wrote.

The unnamed reporter's tone went from awe at having landed such a fantastic assignment—he reports he stayed until all his money was spent—to outright indignation.

Marie Gomez was so proud of her brothel that she had her name set out in tiles (demolished).
CURT LANG PHOTO, 1972. VPL 85872X

"Take this from us: Alexander Street at its worst was never as open as it is now. It certainly seems rotten that in defiance of all law and order, this place is allowed to run. The people can thank the Attorney General's department for the continuance of this evil in this city of Vancouver."

By 1914, anxieties about white slavery came to the forefront again as moral crusaders feared that white girls were fraternizing with Chinese men, and police swooped down on Alexander Street. The prisoner records of October 1914 are filled with arrests of brothel keepers and inmates from the area. But while Alexander Street was no longer an unofficial red light district, it never really shut down entirely.

KIYOKO TANAKA-GOTO
35 West Hastings Street

Kiyoko Tanaka-Goto was an enterprising Japanese woman who was born in Tokyo and came to Canada in 1916 as a 20-year-old "picture bride." A picture bride was a forerunner to a mail order bride. Men who were too poor to travel to Japan to select their own brides would send their pictures to a matchmaker who would facilitate a marriage.

Tanaka-Goto spent a few years on Vancouver Island, scratching out a living by milking cows, cleaning out chicken coops and taking in laundry. It's not clear what happened to her husband, but by 1920 she'd saved up $2,000, moved to Vancouver and bought into a brothel at the corner of Powell and Gore with three other women.

"We didn't have a liquor licence and there was singing and dancing and a lot of noise all the time so we got hustled by the police fairly often," she told *Opening Doors* in 1978. "The first year of the business was so good I couldn't believe it. There weren't many women around then and a lot of our customers were fishermen and loggers. I made a lot of money."

In 1927 Tanaka-Goto leased a floor of 35 West Hastings Street from the Palace Hotel. The main floor was a medical clinic and Tanaka-Goto turned the upstairs

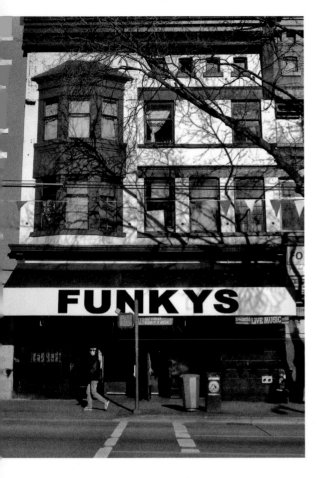

into a brothel, justifying the business by saying that buying the lease, expensive rent, and only having 35 rooms made it impossible to make a profit if it was run as a hotel. She hired 12 prostitutes and took 30 percent of their earnings, instead of the usual 50 percent commission. White woman, she noted, went for $2, while the more exotic Japanese between $3 and $5.

Tanaka-Goto's role was to be friendly towards customers and the police. If a police officer wanted a girl, he got her for free and the house paid the girl. It was just the cost of doing business.

In 1942, Tanaka-Goto was one of the 22,000 Japanese Canadians rounded up and interned in British Columbia's Interior. On her return to Vancouver four years later, she tried running various gambling, bootlegging and prostitution rings out of a couple of different Powell Street buildings, but it was never the same.

"Everything's changed since the war and the police are much tougher," she said. "I couldn't get a licence, and although I still served sake in a teapot, I lost a lot of money."

None of the madams had anything on the real estate of Joe Celona, who was known as the King of the Bawdy Houses and the Mayor of East Hastings. Celona was the largest operator in the city. During the years he spent in Vancouver, Celona managed to bring down one mayor and two police chiefs.

In 1927 Kiyoko Tanaka-Goto ran her brothel from the top floor of what was then the Palace Hotel.
EVE LAZARUS PHOTO

JOE (ANTONIO) CELONA (1897–1958)
4973 Angus Drive

Joe Celona arrived in Vancouver in 1919, moved into 272 Union Street, and opened up a cigar store a couple of blocks away at Main and Keefer. Celona wanted a more profitable way to make money than selling cigars, and soon had his tentacles into bootlegging, prostitution and gambling—often all three in the same establishment.

In an anonymous letter sent to the police chief in May 1922, translated from Italian by Detective Joe Ricci, the correspondent wrote that Celona had six of the youngest and prettiest girls working for him on Union Street.

"This affair is protected by your men who go and come at their convenience by the back door. Sometimes they get drunk to show they are true friends of this boss. They bring women from other quarters to this house. If there is fear of being raided, your men tell the boss to stop for a few days."

Celona's first sentence came in June 1922, when he was hauled off to jail for turning his Union Street home into a brothel.

It was a small price to pay. Bootlegging through the BC Prohibition years had made him rich, and the conviction just made him careful.

In 1924, Celona moved into his new house in upmarket Shaughnessy. While the house is a sturdy looking craftsman, it was no mansion. His guest list, though, was

impressive. Mayor L.D. Taylor was one of a number of guests who saw in the New Year at the Celona's home.

By 1924 Joe Celona made enough money from bootlegging and brothels to build his Shaughnessy house. EVE LAZARUS PHOTO

Celona sold the Union Street property in 1928 and was soon openly operating brothels at various times at 210 Keefer Street, the Maple Hotel at 177 East Hastings, the Windsor Hotel at 52 East Hastings, the Howard Hotel at 124 East Hastings, the Morgan Building at 242 East Hastings, and rooms at 513 Main Street.

At the 1928 Lennie Commission into police corruption, Mayor L.D. Taylor testified that he only knew Celona as the proprietor of a cigar shop on Main Street. Ivan Ackery, a well-known theatre manager, remembered it somewhat differently. In his memoir *Fifty Years on Theatre Row*, Ackery wrote that Mayor Taylor would take over the Belmont Cabaret every Sunday evening to entertain his friends. Joe Celona, he said, provided the booze and the women.

"Six nights a week the public danced to Les Crane and his orchestra, but the seventh night belonged to his Honor."

Celona's brothels were colour blind and catered to both a white and a Chinese clientele. When he felt that officers were harassing his business, Celona went straight to the mayor, who took the complaint to the chief and had police back off. He wasn't doing Celona any favours though, testified the Mayor; on the contrary, he felt it was a dangerous thing to break in doors without a warrant.

Taylor's concerns were likely justified. At the same Commission, Detective Joe Ricci testified how he had raided Celona's brothel at 210 Keefer in 1926.

"One time I fooled him. I happened to have a false warrant and I shoved it under his door and told the landlady to open the door or I would break it in," Ricci said. "She read the warrant and the door was opened. I went in and got what I wanted."

Detectives, said Ricci, were merely a collection agency for the city. They were told to go from place to place, make the odd raid and arrest the prostitutes from time to time, releasing them a short time later.

Ricci reeled off the addresses of a dozen brothels operating on Union, Keefer, Prior, East Hastings and Alexander Streets and said: "If I had anything to do with it. I would drown them all. I would have nothing to do with those class of people."

CHIEF CONSTABLE JOHN CAMERON
1591 West 29th Avenue

Joe Celona's relationship with law enforcers stayed cozy into the 1930s. He was pals with Chief of Police John Cameron—the same officer who lost an eye in the Malcolm MacLennan shooting of 1917. Cameron left the Vancouver Police Department in 1929 to take over the helm of New Westminster's police department. Living well beyond his salary, he built a majestic 4,000 square foot Georgian Revival house at 431 3rd Street in New Westminster for himself and his new wife Kathea. When the City of New Westminster returned Cameron to Vancouver in 1933, he moved into an equally splendid Shaughnessy house on a corner block on West 29th Avenue.

His reign as police chief was short and disastrous.

By 1935, Cameron was on the wrong side of the court room facing charges of corruption. A police investigation found that Celona was seen at Cameron's

Shaughnessy home and at his ranch near Port Haney. Celona had brought bottles of booze to his office, and they had both cruised around Howe Sound in a police boat, sipping cocktails and being entertained by a piper from the police band.

Cameron beat the charge, but Celona was hauled off to court for another sensational trial. Now 38, he was convicted of procuring two servant girls aged 16 and 21 to work at his brothel on the top floor of the Maple Hotel on East Hastings. What horrified the witnesses at the trial was not that the girls were prostituting themselves, but that they were prostituting themselves with Asian men.

CELONA BACK IN JAIL

At Celona's trial, prosecutor Dugald Donaghy charged: "The case would have been bad enough if the girls had prostituted themselves with white men," he said. "But no words are too abhorrent to characterize the procuring of girls to submit to the embraces of crawling, vermin, yellow beasts."

Represented by Stuart Henderson, veteran criminal court barrister, Celona answered questions in a strong Italian accent. Reporters described him as "urbane, bespectacled and dressed in expensive blue tweed." He was out on $30,000 bail, but it was short-lived and he was soon back in jail serving an 11-year jail sentence.

The trial brought Mayor L.D. Taylor down for a second time. Gerry McGeer, a well known lawyer and politician who had played a quasi-prosecution role in the Lennie Commission of 1928, ran against him for mayor on a mandate to fight crime. He vowed that he would rid the city of gambling, white slavery and corruption in the police force. One of his favourite slogans was "we're going to Barcelona (bar Celona)."

After he was released from jail, Celona resumed his businesses. In 1955 he was hauled in again to testify at the Mulligan Affair. A short time later he told a reporter: "There's no dough left in bootlegging. All the bawdyhouses are closed. Now they stop a man taking a few honest bets."

Celona died in 1958 from colon cancer. His death certificate says he was a divorced proprietor of a rooming house living at 193 West King Edward—quite a slide from his former Shaughnessy address.

opposite top: Chief Constable John Cameron in 1934, shortly before going on trial for corruption. STUART THOMSON PHOTO. CVA 99-2828

opposite bottom: Chief John Cameron's swanky Shaughnessy house would have been unaffordable on a cop's salary. EVE LAZARUS PHOTO

below left: In 1935 Joe Celona was convicted of procuring young girls to work at his brothel in the Maple Hotel. CVA HOT N65

below right: The Windsor Hotel was one of Joe Celona's brothels in 1931. CVA 99-3884

CHAPTER 4

Take a Walk on the Wild Side

opposite: 830 Union Street.
EVE LAZARUS PHOTO

below: Lucille Mars, July 1956.
PHOTO COURTESY OF JUDY MAIDA

"*Crime is violence. Crime is not bootlegging from a home. Crime is not prostitution from a home. Crime is destruction; destruction of homes, of goods of people, of community. Crime is power and progress in the form of a bulldozer tearing down family homes and replacing them with cheap concrete housing projects, crime is neighbourhoods lost to super freeways.*"
—Ines Leland, in *Opening Doors*, 1978.

LUCILLE MARS
830 Union Street

Lucille Mars was born in 1920 at the back of an old bootlegging shack in Gastown, helped into the world by a woman named French Marie. Karolina Fedychyn, 48, emigrated from Russia in 1912, and Lucille was her eleventh child. Two years later Fedychyn married Anton Eletz, a worker at the Sitka Spruce Lumber Company and they bought a two-storey Edwardian house on Union Street.

There were always boarders in the house, and in the 1930s men were stacked six deep in the three upstairs bedrooms, two to a double bed and two on the cots. Lucille and two of her sisters shared a bed in a room under the stairs. Fedychyn worked in a coal factory down by the CNR and sewed sacks in a house on East Georgia. She charged a penny for a gunny sack and two cents for a coal sack. Like most of the families in the area, the Fedychyns bootlegged red wine and whisky.

The Fedychyn kids made money where they could. At age 10, Lucille was tap dancing and playing the mouth organ at the corner of Main and Prior Streets in the hopes of spare change. After school and on weekends, the kids could often make some money running errands for the madams in the brothels along Gore and Union Streets. If they were lucky, one of the visiting clients would flick them a silver dollar.

When they collected some money, Lucille and her friends would head down to spend it at the general store a few doors down from their house. Built as a Chinese laundry in 1913, 810 Union Street became a grocery store in the late 1920s and was widely known to serve ice-cream from the front of the store while bootlegging booze from the back.

THE MILE OF VICE

By the 1930s, Vancouver was deep into an economic depression. Desperation, combined with antiquated liquor laws, allowed Vancouver's bootlegging industry to flourish. Union Street east of Main became known as the "Mile of Vice" for the large number of bootleggers and brothels in the area. Most of the bootlegging joints were family-run, home-based businesses and the prostitution evolved out of a strong sense of self-preservation.

It was a place where the west side folk would come to walk on the wild side. It was so notorious that in 1930, Union Street east of Vernon Drive was renamed Adanac (Canada spelt backwards) so homeowners could disassociate themselves from the street's reputation.

It was often an uneasy relationship for the Dry Squad. Many cops like Joe Ricci and Bernie Smith had grown up on the east side and understood the challenges that faced immigrant families. Louise Ricci says her father told her that while he'd go after the big players, he'd often leave the families alone. "They used to have the stills underneath the steps on Union Street to distill alcohol," she says. "My dad used to say to his partner 'just leave the lady alone. She has to have some money to feed the kids, let's look the other way.'"

446 Union Street

Like dozens of Italian families in the area, the Piovesans bootlegged their way through the Depression. The family made beer and wine in the European tradition and bought rum from the government-run liquor store, which they then resold in shots. Drinks sold for a dime, while a glass of bucaro, a wine usually made from raisins and the mash of a better wine, sold for a nickel. The family didn't have much of a choice. The Piovesans had built themselves the brick house on Union Street in 1930 just in time to see the economy collapse. A little later, Star Cabs, the taxi company that Adam Piovesan co-owned, went broke. Adam was a longshoreman, but work was scarce and fiercely competitive.

Bootlegging was a stressful existence. The Piovesan's had been raided once and Maria had to pay a $300 fine—a massive amount of money that forced the family to bootleg more liquor to pay it.

"You were always on your toes waiting for something to happen," says Gilda, the oldest daughter.

Gilda remembers a colourful crowd of customers. There was Kitty the Bitch, Gumboot Annie, Shortie the Painter, Jimmy the Corker, and the Spaniard from the area, a stream of loggers from the camps, and railway workers arriving by taxi.

In 1944, the Piovesans moved out of the area to a bigger place on Franklin Street and sold their Union Street house to Wally "Blondie" Wallace and his wife Nellie Maida.

The Piovesans were small-time bootleggers driven by need. Wally "Blondie" Wallace was one of the largest bootleggers in the area.

"We'd stake the place out and grab the cars as they came out," said Bernie "Whistling" Smith. "He'd have four or five drivers, and they'd be at all different places and they'd have cheap cars in case they got caught."

The first time a bootlegger was caught they were fined. The second time they went to jail. If they were caught with liquor in the car, both the liquor and the car became the property of the crown. Smith said that around 1950, Wallace had just bought a new Chrysler when he was arrested for bootlegging from his car and sent up to Oakalla prison for three months.

"Hugh Christie was the warden and when they seized the car, they gave the car to the warden, and there's Blondie Wallace watching the warden drive his car," said Smith.

Wallace was a neighbourhood hero, dodging the cops in his bootlegging operation by night and teaching the kids to box in the basement of his house during the day. He operated a thriving distribution centre from the garage just off a lane at the back of the house, and ran Wallace Transfer out of an old Union Street garage.

"That's how he got caught," says Judy Maida. "He bought a whole fleet of moving and storage trucks and paid cash and they got him for income tax evasion because how does a guy who doesn't make any money, all of a sudden put out $100,000 for trucks?"

Judy is Blondie Wallace's niece by marriage. She grew up surrounded by bootleggers. Her father ran a taxi company on the North Shore, and used to deliver the bottles in the cab all over the Lower Mainland. "My father used to hide it in a graveyard, and he'd go out at night and go get it," she says.

above: Wally "Blondie" Wallace operated a distribution centre from his garage and a trucking company on Union Street.
PHOTO COURTESY JUDY MAIDA

below: The Maida's ran a bootlegging business from their house on Union Street.
EVE LAZARUS PHOTO

836 Union Street

Judy says she knew husband-to-be Rick Maida for a while before she realized he was similarly connected to the business of bootlegging. When they first met she recalls that he was always busy on Sunday nights and on long weekends. "After we were dating for a while he said I can't tell you exactly what I'm doing, but I'm busy," she says. "Then after months of going out he gave me a business card and I thought maybe he was a pimp or something, and he said you can't tell anybody my family are bootleggers. I said to him 'Oh my god, my father and my grandfather were bootleggers!'"

The business card had a picture of a cowboy, and a phone number. It introduced the bearer as a "member of our Pistol Club: You may drink till 2:00."

Judy and Rick were married in 1969.

Rick worked for his mother, Marie "Mary" Nunsiatta—Nellie Wallace's sister-in-law. Mary took over Wally Wallace's bootlegging business after his death in 1965 and after her husband, a car salesman, hurt his back and couldn't work.

She initially operated her bootlegging business out of their home at 836 Union Street, and later moved her home and business to College Street.

Bootlegging, always a constant presence in Vancouver's history, took many forms. Sometimes it operated out of somebody's house, other times as a blind pig. And there were opportunities for other people to make some money by delivering booze after the bars closed.

The Maida's was a family business. At one point it employed Rick, his mother, his younger brother, and an uncle as drivers. Nunsiatta would buy a case of beer from the government-run liquor store for around $2.50 and sell it for $5. She'd split the profit with the driver.

Largely because of bizarre liquor laws that saw liquor stores shut early and close on weekends, bootlegging enterprises like the Maida's continued right into the 1970s.

Judy says they used to hide up to 50 cases of beer in the attic at College Street. The "good stuff" went into Mary's old oak table. The table, which had been her mother's, had a huge round hollow base and was perfect for hiding booze in the event of a raid.

"Bernie Smith busted my mother-in-law in the '70s, shortly after my husband and I got married," says Judy. "I was there for Sunday dinner and we were in the kitchen making spaghetti and my mother-in-law was answering the phones at the same time and taking orders, and my husband saw two men with policemen haircuts coming through the yard across the alley."

Rick yelled "dry squad," jumped into his car and hit the accelerator. There was so much dust from the un-paved lane that officers called in the wrong colour car, said Judy. Rick's father-in-law wasn't so lucky. His car wouldn't start, and when police searched it and found liquor, they took the booze and the car with them.

Ironically, a few years after Wally's death in the 1960s, Nellie married Mel Spotswood, a Vancouver Police officer on the Dry Squad. Spotswood died in 1974 from alcoholic cirrhosis.

PALMIRA BEZZASSO
620 Keefer Street

When Palmira Bezzasso arrived in Canada in 1914, she had no education, no money, and no English. She also had a deadbeat husband who she had promised her mother she'd marry. By the time her husband returned to Italy three years later, they had two small children, and Palmira elected to stay.

Palmira was the oldest of 13 brothers and sisters and grew up in a two-bedroom shack with a dirt floor in Italy. She felt it was her responsibility to take care of all of her family. She moved into a house at 626 Prior Street, cleaned houses for the rich in Shaughnessy, and ran a prosperous bootlegging business from her house.

By 1937, she had saved up enough money to buy the Keefer Street house.

Palmira's house is one of the biggest in Strathcona and uncommonly fancy for the area. It has a large foyer, a double wide sweeping staircase at the entry, stained glass throughout, five bedrooms and a servant's staircase at the back. William Cline built the house in 1902, for John Addyman Clandening, a foreman at Hastings Mill. The cost to build the house was $2,000, about four times the cost of an average house in Strathcona at the time.

Palmira turned the Clandening's home into a boarding house, but it was still a tough existence. Bootlegging was her salvation: not only was it lucrative, but it was one of the few industries available to women in the 1930s.

Joy Bezzasso, Palmira's granddaughter, remembers growing up in a house filled with boarders, visitors, and others who drifted down from the logging and mining camps looking for a drink and good company.

"There was always something going on," says Joy. "We had boarders, we had people coming from Italy because they stopped here and then they got themselves together, got a job, got themselves some money, and then they moved on."

Palmira bought liquor from the government run stores and she also made her own. Joy and her brother helped Palmira make red wine in the basement.

"We had barrels and wine making stuff and we would stomp on the grapes with our gumboots because my grandmother said it was more sanitary."

Joy remembers lying in bed as a little girl—the same room she sleeps in now—keeping as still as possible while the police went through her drawers and cupboards and searched under her bed for alcohol. "We would get raided

all the time, it was really devastating as a child," she said. "I grew up thinking that the police were the bad guys."

When Joy was nine the police arrested her 74-year-old grandmother for the third time, and this time they sent her off to Oakalla Prison to serve out a six-month sentence.

"When she came back she was happy as can be, and I asked her why. She said it was the first time in her life that somebody actually cooked for her and brought her meals," said Joy. "She said it must have been like Hollywood because in Hollywood they treat you like a queen, and they treated her like a queen in jail."

Palmira passed her time in jail knitting, and Joy still has the little doll her grandmother made in the living room, propped up next to the boarding pass of the ship on which Palmira sailed from Italy.

Palmira died in 1974, aged 94. Joy is determined that her family will continue to benefit from her grandmother's generosity and her legacy. In February 2013, Joy had two coach houses built in the back for her two grandsons. She had her house designated as a heritage building to ensure its survival.

"It wasn't about money for my grandmother," says Joy. "It was about survival at first, and then being able to help others, that's all she cared about and making sure that everybody else was looked after."

above: The doll that Palmira knitted in Oakalla Prison. EVE LAZARUS PHOTO

below: Boy riding past the Union Laundry in 1973 - 272 Union on left (demolished). CVA 203-65

opposite top: Jimi Hendrix shrine, 207 Union Street (renumbered #209). EVE LAZARUS PHOTO

opposite bottom: Nora Hendrix bought her East Georgia Street house in 1934. EVE LAZARUS PHOTO

THE PADLOCK WAR

Raids, arrests, fines and court convictions failed to stop the East End bootleggers or deter their customers. So in June 1937, a frustrated city magistrate came up with the innovative idea of ordering police to padlock the homes of the most notorious operators.

Reporters followed police from house to house as they clamped on the padlocks at Dominic Caruso's and Louis Mattlo's Union Street homes, and at Tony Borsato's West End home. What the police and the judge didn't anticipate was that the bootleggers and their families would refuse to leave.

It made for great headlines, photos and copy, such as in this *Vancouver Sun* story. "Before the padlock was applied to rear and front of the house, Caruso arrived. Nattily attired in a dapper gray suit and fedora, Dominic strolled up the front steps. With a waving of arms, Caruso vehemently told the officer to go ahead and apply the padlock, that he and his family would stay inside."

Caruso, who lived in Joe Celona's former digs at 272 Union Street, told Inspector Tuning not to worry, he'd chop down the door if he needed to get out.

The Dry Squad officers climbed into their autos and drove to the Borsato's. Mrs. Borsato and her three-year-old daughter Rena hurried out to buy three bottles of milk before police snapped on the padlock.

When Louis Mattlo arrived home to find his Union Street house padlocked, he borrowed a screwdriver and tried to force his way in through the front door. He was arrested and hauled off to the police station.

Unfortunately, police had locked in the Mattlo family tabby and had to go back in to rescue the cat.

Uniformed officers were posted outside each of the homes to help facilitate the departure of the family members should they change their minds. They didn't.

The siege lasted for over two weeks, with Dominic Caruso, described as a "fiery little Italian with an Englishman's notion of his home being his castle," being the last hold-out.

The padlocked houses have long since been demolished, but before Mattlo's house was turned into a parking lot in the 1970s, the building housed Vie's Chicken and Steak House, a famous Hogan Alley landmark operated by Vie and Robert Moore for more than 30 years.

Vie's became a favourite destination for visiting black performers including Nat King Cole and Louis Armstrong.

Local legend has it that Nora Hendrix worked at Vie's and that her grandson, rocker Jimi Hendrix (1942-1970), visited there and perhaps even played there. Jimi Hendrix fans converted a small red building next door at 207 Union Street, now renumbered 209, into a shrine for the rock star.

NORA HENDRIX
827 East Georgia Street

Nora was born in Tennessee. She was a dancer in a vaudeville troupe that travelled across North America. She married Ross Hendrix, a former Chicago cop, and settled in Vancouver in 1911. Their first address was 783 East Pender. Nora and Ross raised three children. Al, the youngest, moved to Seattle at age 22. In Seattle he met 16-year-old Lucille, and their son Jimi was born there in 1942.

Nora bought the house on East Georgia Street in 1934, four years after Ross died, and she lived there until 1952. Jimi was a frequent visitor.

According to *Jimi Hendrix, the Man, the Magic, the Truth*, a biography published in 2004, Jimi lived in 14 different places, including short stints in Vancouver.

"I'd always look forward to seeing Gramma Nora, my dad's mother in Vancouver, usually in the summer," he once told author Sharon Lawrence. "I'd pack some stuff in a brown sack, and then she'd buy me new pants and shirts and underwear. I kept getting taller and growing out of all my clothes, and my shoes were always a falling-apart disgrace."

Shortly after Hendrix left the army in 1962, he hitchhiked 2,000 miles to Vancouver and stayed several weeks with Nora. He picked up some cash sitting in with a group at a club known as Dante's Inferno. Six years later, when the Jimi Hendrix Experience played the Pacific Coliseum, one reviewer described the band as "bigger than Elvis." Hendrix, dressed in all white, played hits such as *"Fire," "Hey Joe,"* and *"Voodoo Child,"* and at one point acknowledged his grandmother who sat in the audience before launching into *"Foxy Lady."*

Nora Hendrix died from breast cancer shortly after celebrating her 100th birthday in 1984.

HARRY HOGAN
406 Union Street

When the Georgia Viaduct plowed through Vancouver in 1972, it knocked out Hogan's Alley, and with it a lot of black history. At one time Hogan's Alley was a hangout and home for Vancouver's black community and filled with after-hours clubs, gambling, prostitution and bootlegging. Just eight feet wide and a few blocks long, the Alley was really just a collection of horse stables, small cottages and shacks.

The alley ran between Union and Prior Streets from Gore to Main Street and was most likely named for Harry Hogan, a black singer who lived in an apartment at 406 Union Street at the corner of Dunlevy in 1921.

The East End also produced its share of writers.

PAUL YEE
540 Heatley Street

Writer and historian Paul Yee lived in three different Strathcona houses between 1960 and 1974.

"I was an orphan," he said. "When whole blocks of houses around me were demolished, I felt like I was being shoved onto a stage for the world to see all the shame that came from living in a slum. Even as a child, I knew Vancouver had better neighbourhoods. I was embarrassed to tell people my address, show others my library card."

opposite: The home of Harry Hogan who was the Hogan in Hogan's Alley.
EVE LAZARUS PHOTO

left: "When I walk through Strathcona now, what really hits me is how green and lush it is," says author Paul Yee. "The place is now respectable, unlike when I lived there."
EVE LAZARUS PHOTO

Yee's first home, 350 ½ East Pender Street is long gone, but the ½ has an interesting history. "The half refers to a smaller house which stood at the rear of the main house behind the fire-wood barn," he said. "Maybe it was meant for servants."

The family left the house in 1968 to live above the Yee's family store at 263 East Pender, and in 1971 they moved to the Heatley Street house.

The house at Heatley and Keefer is a simple three-storey stucco house that sits at street level. After the Heatley address, and following the pattern of many immigrants, the Yee's moved east into the Grandview Woodlands neighbourhood.

Yee, a third-generation Chinese Canadian who now lives in Toronto, has written a number of award-winning children's books as well as *Saltwater City: an Illustrated History of the Chinese in Vancouver*. He says that while the need to escape his childhood neighbourhood is reflected in his adult life, when he returned to Strathcona he was shocked at the change.

"When I walk through Strathcona now, what really hits me is how green and lush it is. All these trees tell me that the place is now respectable, unlike when I lived there."

WAYSON CHOY
630 Keefer Street

The East End is the setting for two of Wayson Choy's award-winning books—*The Jade Peony*, published in 1995, and his 1999 memoir *Paper Shadows: a Chinatown Childhood*. Choy was born in 1939. His mother was a meat cutter and sausage stuffer in a Chinatown factory, and his father cooked onboard Canadian Pacific ships. When he was six, the family moved to the Edwardian house on Keefer Street. When he was 56 he found out, quite by accident, that he was adopted. The only detail he could find out about his biological parents was that his father was a member of the Cantonese Opera Company in Vancouver.

left: Author Wayson Choy lived in this Keefer Street house in the 1940s. EVE LAZARUS PHOTO

The two-storey house has a bay window, a pretty stained glass flower motif in the front left-hand corner, a front porch, and Doric columns. The house nestles between a Vancouver Special on one side, and a home at 636 Keefer Street which was once the Good Shepherd Mission. Choy moved to Toronto in 1962. In 2005, he was named a member of the Order of Canada.

URBAN RENEWAL

By 1958, the Chinese were being frozen out of their homes. City Planners declared Strathcona a "slum" and slated it for demolition. "Urban renewal" became the new buzzword, and one that would save the residents from themselves. As part of the city's urban renewal plan for Strathcona, the city froze property values, stopped any regular public works maintenance in the area and stopped issuing any redevelopment or home improvement permits. Many of these Chinese homeowners lived in extended families, and urban renewal would split up the families and see them stashed into soulless subsidized public housing.

The first phase, in 1969, saw 30 acres bulldozed to make way for the MacLean Park high-rise and the Raymur-Campbell Public Housing Project. Three years later, the city's $17 million second phase went ahead, displacing 2,300 people, mostly Chinese. Then the city announced a plan to construct a freeway between Union and Prior Streets. Connected via a new Georgia Viaduct, the freeway would carve up parts of Chinatown and Gastown with the freeway hub located at Pender and Carrall Streets in Chinatown.

This wholesale uprooting and destruction of the area continued until November 1968, when 600 local residents led by Mary Chan founded the Strathcona Property and Tenants Association (SPOTA).

MARY CHAN
658 Keefer Street

Mary Chan almost single-handedly drummed up the support needed to save her neighbourhood. Shirley Chan remembers accompanying her mother while she knocked on doors, talked, cajoled, and canvassed donations to hire a lawyer to take on City Hall. The Chans held early organizing meetings in their large Edwardian house. Later the meetings moved between the Chan household, Harry Con's house at 329 East Pender, the First United Church, and Chinatown restaurants.

Mary was born in Vancouver in 1915, the third of 10 children. When the government announced the Chinese Immigration Act in 1923, the struggling family gave up and moved back to China. Mary was eight. There, she married Walter Chan, a teacher. In 1947, after the Act was lifted, she returned on her own to Canada, pregnant with Shirley. Mary worked three jobs, mostly in fish canneries and Gas-

Georgia and Dunsmuir ramps over Main Street, 1971. Photo shows Vie's Chicken and Steak House, next to building at Main and Union.
CVA 216-1.23

51

town clothing factories, until she had enough money to bring her husband to Canada. By 1955, they had saved enough money to buy the Keefer Street house.

Soon after moving into their house, the Chans learned about the urban renewal program. Thinking that if they fixed up their house, they'd be able to keep it, they hired people to do repairs. Then they discovered that the entire neighbourhood was to be demolished.

"Mom had a natural organizing ability," said Shirley Chan, herself a highly regarded community activist, urban planner and government administrator. "Whenever there was any issue that was important, Mom would drag me around after work or on weekends, and my job was to translate for her, except I never had to translate because she always did all the talking herself anyway. She was just afraid she might not understand something."

Shirley's brother Larry Chan says their mother was known as the "Field Marshall."

"She was a big strong woman willing to use physical force and manual labour to accomplish things and she was the perfect opposite of my father, he being quiet and academically accomplished," he says. "In meetings my mother would pound the table to get people's attention and then address everybody with a loud voice to make her point.

My father would have people stop and ask him for his thoughts. They worked well together that way. It was very effective."

In 1969, the planners at City Hall organized a tour for federal Minister of Housing Paul Hellyer. He invited Shirley to go with him on the bus. "I had an opportunity to show him these houses that were still true. Okay the porch might need to be replaced, but the fact is it was still decent, safe, affordable housing for these families." He returned to Ottawa and announced a freeze on urban renewal.

"It was a tremendous victory and we used opportunities like this to bring the community together and know that we had achieved something special to have stopped urban renewal and changed national housing policy," said Shirley.

Mary died in 2002, and her son Larry Chan, a Vancouver naturopathic doctor, now owns the three-storey family home.

"Personally, I would like my own children to realize the important role that my parents had in preserving Strathcona," he said.

The story of Strathcona is one of survival. Its early inhabitants were mostly British working class immigrants, which over time changed to Japanese, Jewish, Russian, Italian, and Chinese immigrants. When they could get work, these early immigrants worked in sawmills, at the railway and at the port. When they couldn't find work, they survived through hard work and ingenuity.

By the 1930s, Vancouver was deep into a depression, and desperation combined with antiquated liquor laws allowed Vancouver's bootlegging industry to flourish. People like Maria Piovesan, Karolina Fedychyn and Palmira Bezzasso were small-time bootleggers. The bigger ones stayed in the wholesaling end of the business, delivering to the clubs, and many made a lot of money selling whisky and beer to the speakeasies, unlicensed clubs, and to high-profile citizens.

Then there were the liquor barons, the truly rich, who made fortunes from their breweries and staggering profits from shipping liquor to the States during Prohibition. The mansions of the liquor barons were, of course, on the west side of town.

opposite top: Walter Chan (middle) and Mary Chan at a Chinese banquet, ca. 1970.
PHOTO COURTESY SHIRLEY CHAN

opposite middle: The Chan family in the back garden at Keefer Street in 1956.
PHOTO COURTESY SHIRLEY CHAN

opposite bottom:
658 Keefer Street in the middle of a massive renovation.
EVE LAZARUS PHOTO, 2014

CHAPTER 5

Built on Rum

B*ritish Columbia introduced Prohibition in 1917, but the experiment was a failure and finished by 1920. It was a different story in the United States, where Prohibition lasted 13 years, paving the way for Canadian entrepreneurs to make heady amounts of money smuggling booze across the border. Rum-running produced a secret society of mariners not adverse to risk and looking for adventure. It wasn't uncommon for a ship to carry bourbon, scotch, rye, gin or rum worth up to $1 million, and a captain could easily rake in $1,000 a trip.*

left: The Commodore Ballroom, ca. 1931. VPL 70488

below: When Captain Robert Pamphlet wasn't running booze down the coast, he lived in this North Vancouver house. EVE LAZARUS PHOTO

CAPTAIN ROBERT PAMPHLET
322 West 6th Avenue, North Vancouver

Captain Robert Pamphlet was riding out a gale just off the mouth of the Columbia River at Astoria, Oregon. He was waiting to unload 1,075 cases of quality whisky. Apart from the storm, Pamphlet wasn't expecting any problems. His two-masted *Pescawha* was an old fishing schooner with a plodding gait of about six knots an hour, but as long as he kept 12 miles between his schooner and the mainland, the risk all belonged to the US-registered speedboats that would deliver the whisky to desperate Americans.

It was the night of February 3, 1925 when Pamphlet took out his binoculars to search for the speedboat. Instead he saw the *Caoba*, a US-based lumber schooner, her masts broken, careening towards the rocks. Close beside it was a lifeboat full of men. Pamphlet alerted his crew, powered up his ship, and swerved across the imaginary boundary between international and US waters to rescue Captain Wilfrid Sandig, eight of his crew and the ship's cat. Unfortunately, Pamphlet was spotted by the US Coast Guard Cutter *Algonquin*. Instead of outrunning the cutter back to

international waters, he hove to and handed over the stranded crewmen. Pamphlet and his crew were arrested, the *Pescawha* impounded and towed to Astoria. The whisky mysteriously disappeared.

Born in Victoria in 1873, Pamphlet came from a seafaring family. His father Tom was captain of the *SS Beaver* and two of his brothers became sea captains. Robert never married, and while not at sea he lived with his brother Fred. Fred was an engineer on the *SS Prince George*, and lived with his family in a large Edwardian house on West 6th.

After his arrest, Pamphlet became a minor celebrity in Vancouver and down the Pacific Northwest coast. The owners of the *Caoba* presented him with a gold watch with the inscription "Capt. Robert Pamphlet, a true sailor, in recognition of his action in rescuing the crew of our SS. Caoba at sea." Thousands of Americans signed a petition asking for leniency, but the American legal system, determined to make an example of him, fined Pamphlet $1,000 and sentenced him to a year at McNeill Island penitentiary near Tacoma.

Pamphlet had a fairly easy time of it. He was assigned to his own cabin and put in charge of captaining the prison boat from McNeill Island to the mainland. He served out his sentence, and then died from tuberculosis in the North Vancouver house in 1931. The *Pescawha*, a former sealing and fishing vessel, sank in a storm two years later.

Liquor manufacturers and mariners weren't the only ones reaping huge profits from US Prohibition. In 1920, the government of BC passed a law legalizing the sale of liquor for export. The act of transporting liquor down to the US was against US law, and crews faced stiff fines and jail terms if caught. However, as long as they paid up their Canadian taxes, the producers and the operators could buy and sell and manufacture all within the law at home.

CONSOLIDATED EXPORTERS
1050 Hamilton Street

Today the Reifels are probably best known for the peaceful Reifel Migratory Bird Sanctuary in Ladner, but few know that the Sanctuary, the old hunting lodge—now the headquarters for the Federal Government's Canadian Wildlife Service—two mansions on Southwest Marine Drive, the Commodore Ballroom, the Vogue and the Studio theatres on Granville Street, were all built from the proceeds of rum-running.

Henry Reifel, a Bavarian-born brewmaster, co-founded the Canadian Brewing & Malting Company in 1908 (now owned by Molson). He was soon joined by his two sons George Conrad and Henry (Harry) Frederick.

By 1920, the Reifels were already supplying rum-runners with their product man-

ufactured from two distilleries and four breweries. In 1922, they became one of several brewery and distillery companies from across the country to form an export house. It was called Consolidated Exporters and was headed up by Captain Charles Hudson. The liquor producers set up their export business in a large warehouse on Hamilton Street in Yaletown, close to the railyards and port facilities needed to supply the smugglers. The Reifels also operated out of 1206 Homer Street, which a number of rum-running ships used as their registered address. These included the Reifel's own fast yacht, *Pleasure,* and the *Ryou 11,* a 60-foot fish packer.

left: Henry Reifel, ca. 1929.
CVA PORT N56

below: The Reifels moved into Rio Vista in 1930. The house came with a conservatory, 10 fireplaces and a sunken ballroom.
EVE LAZARUS PHOTO

Consolidated Exporters was an early example of vertical integration. It was a textbook example of what happens when a manufacturer owns its suppliers and distributors, handles sales and finances, and in doing so, reduces costs and risk. Rum-running was also an economic generator for the port of Vancouver, as great sums of money were spent on building boats, maintaining engines, outfitting ships with food, supplies and fuel, and employing crews and dock workers.

By the late 1920s, supplying rum to thirsty Americans became so lucrative for the Reifel family that George and Harry were able to build massive houses on large acreages along Southwest Marine Drive, alongside bluebloods like W.H. Malkin, wholesale grocer and future mayor of Vancouver, George Kidd, the general manager of BC Electric Railway, and Gordon Farrell, president of BC Telephone Corp.

RIO VISTA

2170 Southwest Marine Drive

Katherine Rempel got her first look at Rio Vista, Harry and Edna Reifel's mansion, one morning in 1932. The 14-year-old girl had immigrated with her family from Orenberg, Russia and settled on a small farm in Abbotsford. The family was struggling through the Depression, and Katherine had moved to Vancouver and was staying at a rooming house run by the Mennonite Church that helped young girls find work.

She answered an interview request from Edna Reifel, who was seeking a German-speaking maid to join her large staff.

A gardener led Katherine past a huge tiled swimming pool, through lavish gardens and past a four-car garage. Sitting high on a bluff above the Fraser River, the house wore a tiled roof, had cast stone ornamentation, a spectacular conservatory, 10 fireplaces, a sunken ballroom, a library with walnut panelling, a billiard room and a full-size tavern.

"There was this beautiful staircase that went round and round and you'd stand there and look down into this foyer," she says. "There were quarters in the basement for the Chinese cook. The ballroom was in the basement."

Katherine worked alongside a cook, two gardeners and a nursemaid for Barbara Ann Mariel and Betty Joan Lorraine. Her room was in the third floor servants' quarters.

"I had to wait on the tables and keep the stairways and entrance clear," she said. "I had very little to do to tell you the truth, it was the best job I ever had."

Following Harry Reifel's death in 1973, Rio Vista sold to Vancouver philanthropist and self-made businessman Joe Segal. He paid $500,000 for the mansion and another $800,000 for Bella Vista, Harry Reifel's Langley farm.

Segal says he was no farmer, but he'd fallen in love with the magnificent craftsmanship and superb quality of Rio Vista in Vancouver. When he put in an offer for Rio Vista he found that a foreign buyer was set to close the deal, not only to buy Rio Vista, but also to purchase the Langley property. "I bought the farm to get the house. The woodwork and the finishings were unbelievable—there was nothing of that quality ever built in the city," he says of Rio Vista.

Segal spent another $1.3 million and two years restoring Rio Vista. As for the farm, he says he hung onto it and farmed it for another five money-losing years before selling it to a group of investors.

Architect Ross Lort designed a hunting lodge on Westham Island for George Reifel in the late 1920s.
EVE LAZARUS PHOTO

THE REIFEL HUNTING LODGE

5421 Robertson Road, Delta

While Harry was building Rio Vista in the late 1920s, his brother George commissioned Vancouver architect Ross Lort to design a hunting lodge at his property on Westham Island, just outside Ladner. An outdoorsman who liked to hunt and fish,

George Reifel had brought associates to the area to hunt ducks and geese since the early 1920s. He bought the land and tidal flats on the south arm of the Fraser River in 1927 and went about creating a complex series of dikes, freshwater sloughs, and large feed areas for the birds. In its heyday as a hunting lodge, the grounds had barns, dog kennels, gardens, a swimming pool and a tennis court.

In 1973, George Reifel Junior sold the waterfowl refuge to the Canadian Wildlife Service for $2.3 million. The parcel included 98 acres that he had previously donated to them on condition that all 1,400 acres remained a wildlife sanctuary and kept the family name.

CASA MIA
1920 Southwest Marine Drive
The senior George Reifel was obviously happy with his hunting lodge because he commissioned Ross Lort to design a flamboyant Spanish-style colonial villa a short distance from Rio Vista. Lort designed Casa Mia, a brightly painted yellow mansion that originally sat on 5.5 acres of land and was clearly visible from both Southwest Marine and from the banks of the Fraser River.

Finished by 1932, the four-level house had over 18,000 square feet of living space, nine fireplaces, 10 bathrooms, a sauna, ballroom, a four-car garage and a full-sized art deco ballroom. In the master bedroom, vaulted ceilings overlooked silk carpets, and there was a gown room with cedar-lined closets and an ensuite bathroom with marble trim. In the middle of rampant unemployment and widespread poverty, George brought up artists from the Walt Disney Studios to hand-paint murals for Jane's third-floor playroom.

The dramatic front entrance way of Casa Mia, built for George Reifel in 1932.
KIM STALLKNECHT PHOTO, 2007
VANCOUVER SUN 23669120

George Reifel died in 1958, and the family sold Casa Mia a decade later to Ross Maclean, a high-profile psychiatrist and hospital owner. A host of Hollywood stars who stayed at his hospital also visited the mansion. Maclean sold the house to Nelson Skalbania in 1980. Skalbania parked his Rolls Royces, his Mercedes-Benz 450 SLs and his prized 1928 Phaeton convertible, used in the motion picture *The Great Gatsby*, in the mansion's multiple garages. A real estate developer who attracted media attention in the late 1970s by flipping property worth millions of dollars, Skalbania at one time owned a $2.7 million de Havilland jet, a 53 metre diesel yacht called Chimon, and sports interests which included the National Hockey League's Atlanta Flames, the Montreal Alouettes, the Vancouver Canadians, and the Edmonton Oilers.

Shortly after Skalbania's spectacular bankruptcy, Casa Mia sold to Bruce Branch and his wife Michiyo, the daughter of a Japanese millionaire, in 1982. Branch hired Ross Lort's son Bill, also an architect, and added another $4.5 million in renovations.

In 2010 Maureen McIntosh and Lynn Aarvold of the Care Group paid $10 million for the mansion in the hopes of retaining the house in return for a change in zoning that would allow a large-scale development for seniors.

Perhaps it was the size of Rio Vista and Casa Mia, their location near the Fraser River, or just the mystery surrounding rum-running in the 1920s and 1930s, but for years there were rumours of tunnels that connected the two houses and led down to the river. Bill Lort, who kept the original house plans, said there were no tunnels in the drawings or any found in the later excavation of the land below the bluff. Likely the Reifels had no need of the subterfuge. They ran legitimate breweries, distilleries and export companies, mostly leased their ships and employed a large number of maritimers to shoulder the risk.

Local lore has it that Alma Reifel, fed up with the crowded Crystal Ballroom of the old Hotel Vancouver, pushed George to build another dance room.

THE COMMODORE BALLROOM
868 Granville Street
In July 2011, *Billboard Magazine* named the Commodore Ballroom one of North America's 10 most influential clubs, right up there with New York's Bowery Ballroom and the Fillmore in San Francisco. The editors didn't mention that the club was built on the proceeds of rum-running.

The art deco building, with its brick façade and terracotta roof, was also the last building that Henry Gillingham would design. The architect suffered a cerebral hemorrhage on a Vancouver streetcar in 1930. He was 55.

On December 3, 1930, the Commodore Cabaret on Granville Street, a two-storey building with a semi-circular bandstand, opened to a sold-out crowd of 1,500. The Commodore started off by booking big bands such as Tommy Dorsey, Rudy Vallée, Count Basie and Dizzie Gillespie and then became a banquet hall during the week and a dance club on Saturday night.

Like other nightclubs and cabarets of that era, the Commodore was what was known as a "bottle club." Customers would sneak in their own bottles of rum and whisky and then pay exorbitant cover charges and, once in, wildly inflated prices for mixers and ice. When the police raided the club, patrons would either stash their booze in secret compartments in the table or just put the bottles on the floor and deny all knowledge of them.

As a detective in the Dry Squad, Bernie Smith spent many nights in and outside of the clubs. "It was part of a way of life, and as a policeman, I didn't feel like crawling on my hands and knees under a table looking for a bottle of whisky, so we would try and get them before they went in," he said. The police took the confiscated liquor to the station, and would later return it to the owner on receipt of a $15 "service charge."

In fact, the Commodore operated for four decades before it finally got a liquor licence.

Nick Kogas and Johnny Dillias ran the Commodore for the Reifel's until 1958 when Doug Gurley, the Reifel's son-in-law, took it over. A decade later Gurley sold

The Commodore Ballroom on Granville Street. Built in 1930.

it to Drew Burns whose hands-on style and eclectic musical tastes brought in sell-out shows for acts such as The Clash, Doug and the Slugs, Bryan Adams and The Police.

Writer and historian Aaron Chapman says that Burns loved jazz and blues, but it was his give-anything-a-try attitude that gave the Commodore its lasting reputation.

"Drew Burns deserves a tremendous amount of credit because he gave a lot of local bands a shot," says Chapman.

Over the next three decades Burns presented thousands of artists, both famous and emerging. He is said to have given k.d. lang her first break, and his office was full of mementoes including a pair of pants that James Brown left behind after a performance and that stayed tossed over a chair for years.

Chapman says that the only time the Commodore closed was for a few months during the Depression, and again after Burns' departure in 1996 when it was closed for three years.

The Vogue Theatre on Granville Street.
PHOTO ©2014 DEREK VON ESSEN

"The local music scene really took a dive in those years," says Chapman. "People would be surprised to learn how close the building came to being gutted, subdivided and turned into retail stores."

After Burns' departure the club went through a series of ownership changes and is now in the hands of Live Nation— one of the largest concert promoters in North America.

THE VOGUE
918 Granville Street

On April 15, 1941, the Dal Richards Big Band was the opening act for the Vogue Theatre, a combination vaudeville and movie house located near the Commodore. A screening of the movie *I See Ice* followed, and nearly 1,400 people filled the Odeon Theatre that night, with almost as many again gathered outside attracted by the spotlights, the lighted marquee, and the huge neon sign.

The day after the opening, the *Vancouver Sun* captured some of the excitement: "Swinging searchlights cut the sky above a gleaming modernistic façade swathed with flags and banners, floodlights glared and hissed, crowds surged against lines held by police and commissionaires, motion-picture cameras whirred and flashbulbs flared, as the guests passed into the theatre, notables among them paused, bowed and spoke brief acknowledgements of introductions into waiting microphones."

Toronto-based Kaplan and Sprachman architects designed the art deco building for Harry Reifel. Inside, the auditorium ceiling was tiered and backlit with neon tubing to resemble waves, and when it first opened, giant golden mermaids were painted on the walls and the washrooms sported art deco aquamarine and orange tiles.

Outside, the Vogue's distinctive neon sign is topped by a 12-foot figure of a kneeling goddess Diana that looks suspiciously like a car hood ornament. She's the second Diana: the first was made of sheet metal and covered in gold leaf by artist Bud Graves and commissioned by Harry Reifel for $500.

When Odeon Theatres renovated the Vogue in the 1960s, the goddess was in rough shape and sent to the scrap heap. A distraught Reifel immediately commissioned a second statue at ten times the price.

"The front of the theatre without her was like a Jersey cow without horns," he told a *Vancouver Sun* reporter at the time.

The sign—one of the largest on theatre row's sea of neon—has changed colours over the years, but is now back to its original red and yellow.

The Vogue Theatre was designated as a national historic site in 1993.

THE STUDIO
919 Granville Street

Seven years after the Vogue Theatre opened, the Reifels built the Studio across the street. The building has undergone several incarnations over the years, including the Eve Theatre in the 1970s, and the Towne Cinema. It is currently a live music venue called Joe's Apartment.

The Studio was designed by Henry Simmonds, an Australian architect, who once had a loose partnership with Ross Lort, the architect who designed George Reifel's Casa Mia. Simmonds developed quite a reputation for designing theatres, including the Stanley Theatre (1930), the now defunct Fraser Theatre, and the Odeon Theatre on Yates in Victoria.

When the Studio opened in 1949 it was Vancouver's first major art theatre. It showed the films of Bergman and Fellini, as well as Japanese films and operatic films. Prices in those early days were 50 cents during the day and 75 cents for evenings and Saturdays.

919 Granville Street.
PHOTO ©2014 DEREK VON ESSEN

ERNIE MCLEOD
3030 Glen Drive

In 1926, Kellsie Barrett was on the deck of a Union Steamship returning to her home in Lang Bay on the Sunshine Coast, when she first laid eyes on Ernie McLeod.

"I looked over and here was this gorgeous creature down at the dock, he had dark curly hair and a tan from somewhere in the South Pacific," she said. "It was love at first sight."

Kellsie was only nine at the time, and McLeod, a 19-year-old artist worked as a deckhand for Stuart Stone on the *Malahat,* a five-masted former First World War naval ship transformed into a rum-runner. The McLeod family spent the summers at the cottage they owned in Lang Bay.

McLeod first went to sea at 12, and later joined the Canadian Merchant Marine. Rum-running was a natural career step.

"It was for the adventure I think and for the money because there was no comparison as to what they could make as a rum-runner with what they could make on legitimate things," she said.

A deckhand on a rum-running boat could easily pull in around $150 a month, about twice the wages of a Vancouver City beat cop.

Kellsie didn't see McLeod again until 10 years later, and by that time Prohibition was over and he had swallowed the anchor. "It means they've stopped going to sea and they've come ashore," she said.

They married in 1936 and moved to Powell River, where McLeod worked at Kelly Spruce, a saw milling company. After the war, they moved to Vancouver and bought the house on Glen Drive.

Jim Stone has the original oil that Ernie McLeod painted of the *Malahat,* a gift to his father Captain Stuart Stone.

Stuart Stone worked for the Reifel family and Consolidated Exporters during Prohibition. In 1929, he was given a $600 per month pay raise and promoted to captain of the *Malahat.* The schooner was known as the Queen of Rum Row when she became a floating warehouse during Prohibition, often packed to the gunwales with 60,000 cases of liquor. She would be anchored in international waters off the coast of Ensenada, Mexico, where her crew would supply a steady stream of customers in speedboats, pleasure crafts and fishing boats who would buy the booze and transport it back to the US mainland.

The Stones lived in Kitsilano and Jim Stone remembers growing up among a tight community of captains and crew members who worked for the Reifel family and lived nearby, including one of the most influential players of the time, Captain Charles Hudson.

above: East Bay #11 under the bow of the Malahat, ca. 1930.
CVA 260.222 JAMES CROOKALL PHOTO

below: Captain Charles Hudson, mastermind of rum row, lived on Waterloo Street from 1926 to 1934.
EVE LAZARUS PHOTO

CAPTAIN CHARLES HUDSON
2828 Waterloo Street

As the marine superintendent of General Navigation Company, Hudson was the mastermind of rum row. He received his Master's papers in 1916, and served in World War I, earning the Distinguished Service Cross while commanding a Q-ship. After the war he moved to Manitoba and took up farming. Fortunately for the rum-running fraternity, he proved to be a lousy farmer and by 1923 he was back in Vancouver making his living from the sea.

"We considered ourselves public philanthropists," Hudson told Ruth Greene, author of *Personality Ships of BC* "We supplied good liquor to poor thirsty Americans who were poisoning themselves with rotten moonshine. We brought prosperity back to the Harbour of Vancouver."

In 1925 Hudson commanded the *Coal Harbour*, but he was most famous for his on-shore activities. He devised a system of coded radio communications for two-way communication between the mother ships and the shore boats that picked up the booze and needed information on coast guard positions before they made their run.

Hudson operated his communications system from a house high on the hill above Jericho Beach.

Rum-running was the Stone's family business. Chet Stone, Stuart's brother, was chief engineer, his brother-in-law Jim Donohue was first officer, and his sister Hazel, Jim's wife, worked as a radio operator for Charles Hudson.

"My aunt Hazel was a very outgoing sort of person, very gregarious. She looked upon it as an adventure," said Jim Stone.

In *My Dad the Rumrunner*, Jim Stone describes what sounds like a modern-day staff retreat, where rum-runners and their families would stay at the Harrison Hot Springs Hotel compliments of the Reifel family, who owned the hotel through their company United Breweries.

Although not in the same league as the Reifels, Joe Hobbs, a Lt. Commander with the Royal Canadian Navy during the First World War, was one of the first to see the potential. He left his ranch in Alberta, became a member of the Royal Vancouver Yacht Club, and set up office in the Standard Building at 510 West Hastings. He began importing spirits from W&A Gilbey's in London and from Scotland's Peter Dawson.

JOSEPH WILLIAM HOBBS (1881–1963)
1656 Laurier Street

It was love at first sight for Joe Hobbs. The *Stadacona*, a gleaming white aristocratic 164-foot steam yacht, with fine lines and a beautifully shaped clipper ship bow, easily outshone every other boat in Esquimalt Harbour. She was christened the *Columbia* in 1898, built for the commodore of the New York Yacht Club to serve as his pleasure yacht. In 1916, she joined the Canadian Navy, was renamed *Stadacona*, and for three years operated out of Halifax as a World War I escort supply ship and as the vehicle of choice for Admiral Sir Charles Kingsmill. After the war she moved to the West Coast and became a patrol vessel in the service of the Canadian Government Department of Fisheries.

In 1924 she became Joe Hobbs' rum-runner.

Joe Hobbs built his Shaughnessy digs in 1925.
EVE LAZARUS PHOTO

Raised on a farm in Newbury, UK, and trained as an engineer, Hobbs was one of Vancouver's more colourful characters. By 1925 he'd made enough money to build a mansion on Laurier in Shaughnessy, where the city's old money lived. He'd founded Hobbs Bros, a ship holding company and front for his smuggling activities, and he added to his business card the respectable title of western vice-president of the Toronto-based G.A. Stimson and Co. Ltd., one of the oldest bond houses in Canada. His job was to oversee the development planned by the company for the Port of Vancouver.

Hobbs bought two yachts. The 100-foot auxiliary schooner *Naden* he bought from the Royal Canadian

Navy in 1924. He refitted her with a four-cylinder gasoline engine, renamed her *Mabel Dell*, and sent her off to the UK to bring home a cargo full of booze destined for the US. He also bought the 150-foot clipper-bowed steam yacht the *Exmouth 11* in England and renamed her *Vencedor*.

He sent *The Stadacona* off to a British shipyard to be refitted for her cargo-carrying life, and named her after the Kuyakuz Mountain in Northern BC. Rum-running ships typically sported bizarre names such as *Adanesne*, *Kitnayakwa*, and *Ououkinsh* in order to throw off the wireless operators for the US Coast Guard. She became *Kuyakuzmt* for short, confounding even her own crew.

3019 Point Grey Road

By 1928, Hobbs was turning legit. He transformed the *Kuyakuzmt* back into a luxury yacht, and called her *Lady Stimson*, presumably after the firm he had recently joined. He divorced his wife Mabel and sold the yacht that he'd named after her to a Hollywood movie star. The steam-powered *Vencedor* sold to Eric Hamber, the newly appointed 13th Commodore of the Royal Vancouver Yacht Club, and future Lieutenant Governor of BC.

right: Joe Hobbs (1881-1963)
CVA 371.64

below: By 1928 Joe Hobbs preferred a house on Point Grey Road with a view of the water.
EVE LAZARUS PHOTO

The following year Hobbs was appointed surveyor of aircraft at Vancouver for the British Corporation Register of Shipping and Aircraft, and according to a profile in the *Sunday Province* in 1930, the old rum-runner was honoured by the admiralty with the rank of lieutenant-commander.

Vancouver was now the third largest city in Canada and was growing in importance in international trade. Hobbs saw Vancouver as a gateway to the Orient and wanted to build a monument to the city. The office tower would be the tallest west of Toronto, graceful, impressive and would dominate the city and the waterfront.

Frederick G. Johnston, president of Stimson's in Toronto, agreed, and saw it as an opportunity to expand the company into Western Canada. With the financing in place, they secured the land at the foot of Burrard and Hastings Street for $300,000 and began to plan the construction of the Marine Building.

Hobbs traded *Lady Stimson* to Willis P. Dewees, general manager of the Strand

Theatre, for Dewees' Point Grey Road house. Built in 1910, by former Vancouver Mayor Alex Bethune, the house is on the waterfront. Hobbs, now 40, could sip his imported Scotch while he watched the construction of the Marine Building from his back porch, with his new bride, 30-year-old divorcee Evelyn Florence Appleyard.

Born in Kentucky, Dewees arrived in Vancouver in 1909 via Oregon. He operated the Princess and the Royal Theatres, and he built the Rex Theatre, which opened in 1913, and ran it until his death in 1949.

Dewees, who had moved a few blocks away to 2815 Point Grey Road, renamed his yacht *Moonlight Maid*.

MARINE BUILDING
355 Burrard Street

Mayor W.H. Malkin blew a golden whistle, lifted the first shovelful of earth, and commenced the groundbreaking for the Marine Building. The event of March 13, 1929, was staged in front of a huge crowd and earned both Hobbs and Stimson's fawning front page coverage in the daily newspapers the next day.

By the following year, public opinion had changed. The building was $1 million over its $1.1 million budget. Detractors called it the "million dollar folly" and said that even though it was situated near the customs house and shipping firms it was in the wrong part of town.

The art deco building was completed several months behind schedule, and cost $2.35 million, and although the Great Depression bankrupted Hobbs and Stimson's, the finished building must have given him immense satisfaction.

It was the first high-rise office tower in the city and the tallest building for more than a decade. And Hobbs proved the detractors wrong. The Marine Building is still one of the most beautiful buildings in Vancouver. It drew the financial district down towards it.

Local firm McCarter and Nairne, the same architects who designed the Harrison Hot Springs Hotel for the Reifels, and the long-gone Georgia Medical-Dental Building, designed an opulent art deco building that celebrated the marine industry, with four of its 22 floors built into the cliff above the waterfront railway tracks.

McCarter and Nairne described the Marine Building as "some great crag rising from the sea, clinging with sea flora and fauna, tinted in sea-green, touched with gold."

The Marine Building was the first high-rise office tower in Vancouver and the tallest building for more than a decade. W.J. Moore's 1935 photo also shows the Quadra Club on West Hastings. CVA BU N7

The building's rooftops are draped with cream terracotta that blends in with the backdrop of the North Shore mountains. Two five-foot terra cotta King Nepunes stand guard from the 16th floor. The building is decorated with crowns and tridents, three-dimensional ships and dozens of different types of aquatic life.

The double revolving doors of the main entrance are surrounded by brass castings of seahorses, turtles, starfish and sea snails and a forest of seaweed. A 40-foot arch has stone murals of famous sailing ships such as Drake's *Golden Hind* of 1577 and McNeill's 1835 *Beaver.* The whole design is capped by bronze Canada geese soaring about the front entrance.

The details of the Marine Building are still jaw dropping, but when it opened in the midst of the Depression, visitors found it so posh that they couldn't get beyond the Grand Concourse—the 90-foot long entrance hall designed to resemble a Mayan temple.

Each of the five elevators had an intricate bronze starburst on their doors and were staffed by some of the city's most beautiful women. With the push of a button, the elevator would travel at 700 feet per minute—nearly five times the normal speed.

McCarter and Nairne moved their offices to the 19th floor and stayed for the next 50 years. Directory listings read like a who's who of business, with tenants that included the Vancouver Board of Trade, Merchants' Exchange, Lloyds Register of Ships, Proctor and Proctor, Safeways, and the American, Ecuadorian, Venezuelan and Costa Rican Consulates. In 1933 there was even a birth control clinic sharing the 16th floor with a number of shipping, grain and manufacturing companies.

At the same time, Vancouver and much of the rest of the world was spiraling into a Depression. Stimson's were in trouble and Hobbs couldn't pay the bills. He offered the building to the City of Vancouver for $1 million, but they turned him down.

Rather fittingly, considering his former rum-running career, in 1933 Hobbs sold his building to the Guinness family for the fire sale price of $900,000.

In 1934, Hobbs moved to Fort William, Scotland and jumped from exporting spirits to making them. Ten years later he bought the Ben Nevis and the Glen Nevis Distilleries, made malt whisky, and gradually rebuilt his fortune. He discovered that a byproduct from his distilleries was protein-rich mash. Hobbs also bought Inverlochy Estates, which included a castle at the foothills of Ben Nevis, the highest mountain in Scotland. Drawing on his earlier experience of ranching in Alberta, he bought close to a thousand head of cattle for his ranch—a scale not seen before in Scotland. He moored his large white yacht in Loch Linnhe.

Known as Old Joe to the locals, Fort William made him a freeman of the city. After his death in 1963, his son (also named Joe) and his Danish wife Grete, took over the 17-bedroom home and turned it into a country hotel. Over the years a host of celebrities stayed there, including Sean Connery, Robert De Niro, Elton John, Barbara Streisand, HRH King Hussein and HRH Queen Noor. In 1989 Grete was named the Hotelier of the Year.

Prohibition was all over by 1933. The following July, Henry Reifel and his sons Harry and George resigned from the board of directors of Brewers and Distillers of Vancouver—the "best known liquor company of the Pacific Coast" because of allegations that their products had found their way south of the border during Prohibition.

THE REIFELS RESIGN

In July of 1933, the *Province* reported that Seattle's Attorney-General had indicted the Reifels and was suing them for a staggering $17.2 million.

The Reifels were accused of bringing over 2,000 cases of assorted liquors, 20 kegs of malt, 12 five-gallon jugs of rum and 74 bottles of "miscellaneous intoxicants." Among the charges were secret landings at Seola Beach, a secluded spot near Oregon, and landing liquor in Seattle without a permit. "The alleged operations included the formation of special companies and the use of a fleet of boats, some of which were directed by radio from British Columbia."

The case eventually settled out of court for $700,000.

The Vancouver Sun

DETECTIVE TRIES TO KILL CUTHBERT SELF

'Missed My Head'

He figured in charges

Mulligan Ouster

... seen in Shakeup

... through gun curtain

Penny twice flying

CHAPTER 6

Ray Munro's Vancouver

"Power tends to corrupt; absolute power corrupts absolutely. Great men are almost always bad men." —Lord Acton

Ray Munro got up from his desk, strapped on his leather shoulder holster and threw on a jacket. Then he and Jack Whelan took a cab to Detective Sergeant Len Cuthbert's house, a modest grey bungalow on the west side of town.

Whelan, a menacing looking ex-wrestler and former police officer, stayed in the cab while Munro rapped on the front door. Cuthbert answered almost immediately. Looking gaunt from worry and lack of sleep, he gestured for Munro to come inside.

"Len," said Munro. "You're in trouble. And unless you get up off your knees and tell either McMorran or the Attorney General the whole goddamn truth, you're going to wind up the fall guy and in jail."

Munro told Cuthbert that he was writing a story that night that would name names. If he didn't go with him, Munro told him, then his other two choices were wait to be arrested, or, and with his typical flair for the dramatic, he opened his coat to reveal a glimpse of his holster, "You can shove yours in your mouth and pull the trigger." (The holster was all for show; Munro's .45 calibre pistol was safely locked away).

It was news that Cuthbert was dreading, but he had no intention of providing more fodder for Munro's stories. He watched from behind the curtain in his living room window as Munro and Whelan sped away.

opposite: Photographer Bill Dennett captures Ray Munro and ex-detective Jack Whelan reading about Len Cuthbert's suicide attempt. VANCOUVER SUN PHOTO

Cuthbert spent another sleepless night. He went to work the next day, sat behind his desk, and at 8:15 that morning, aimed his .38 calibre service revolver at his chest and pulled the trigger. The bullet missed his heart by a fraction of an inch.

It was June 24, 1955.

A HISTORY OF CORRUPTION

History books typically show Vancouver as a pioneer city built on forestry, fisheries, and tourism, but behind the snow-capped mountains and rainforests the Vancouver of the first half of the 20th century was a seething mass of corruption.

The top job at the Vancouver Police Department was a revolving door, with scandal after scandal ending police careers. Since the city's incorporation in 1886, the police force had seen seven decades of probes, charges of graft and corruption, firings and dissension. The average tenure for a police chief was four years.

The first major scandal came when charges of bribery and corruption were laid at the Lennie Commission of 1928. Police Chief Henry Long, his deputy, Detective Inspector George McLaughlin, and Mayor L.D. Taylor all came in for criticism. Long and McLaughlin were thrown out of their jobs, and the mayor lost an election later that year.

In 1934, Joe Celona, dubbed the King of the Bawdy Houses by the press of the day, and Police Chief John Cameron were brought up on conspiracy charges. Celona was thrown in jail; Cameron lost his job.

Twelve years later, back in the mayor's office again, McGeer did another housecleaning of the force after a scandal involving bribery charges.

In 1952 it was standing room only once again at the Law Courts as the bookie conspiracy case played out, but it was the Mulligan Affair of 1955 that really captured the country's attention.

It's amazing it took so long. In the years between 1949 and 1952 three detective sergeants—Len Cuthbert, Archie Plummer and Bob Leatherdale—had taken their evidence of Chief Walter Mulligan's corruption to the Police Commission and City Prosecutor Gordon Scott. The men were told their complaints would be investigated.

Nothing was done.

Vancouver of the 1950s was still filled with after-hours gambling joints, bootleggers thrived and drugs were once again taking a heavy toll. But it wasn't until the 1954 gangland execution of drug dealer Danny Brent and the attention from Senator Tom Reid that the spotlight started to shine on Mulligan.

Reid's report stated: "Where law enforcement is lax, that's where you find the big traffic in dope. In narcotics, Vancouver is Canada's capital."

Ray Munro, a reporter with the *Province*, was becoming increasingly frustrated with the mainstream newspapers' reluctance to report on corruption in the Vancouver Police Department. He suspected top cop Walter Mulligan was on the take and that police officers took bribes and routinely looked the other way. When a senior police officer and trusted source told him that Mulligan was taking bribes, Munro decided to act.

He quit his job at the *Province* and took his story to *Flash*, a *National Enquirer*-style tabloid based in Toronto. In one of his first stories, the headline screamed: "Rape of Vancouver! Munro tears mask from crooked law in gangland Eden." The text followed: "A police chief who took a piggy bank—a deputy chief whose secret activities and fits of rage are the talk of a neighbourhood—crooked detectives and enough intrigue to make the fictitious Mike Hammer look like a Lavender Lad—that's the talk of this port city today!"

Expecting heavy sales, *Flash* had printed 10,000 extra copies. Every copy sold.

The public charges of graft and corruption finally kicked the Police Commission into action, and Reginald Tupper, QC, was appointed to head up a Royal Commission to once again look into corruption in the Vancouver Police Department.

REGINALD HIBBERT TUPPER (1893–1972)
2810 Southwest Marine Drive

The appointment of Reggie Tupper took a lot of the legal community by surprise. Tupper, the grandson of Sir Charles Tupper, a former Prime Minister of Canada, was a member of the law firm that his father had co-founded—and that still exists today as Bull, Housser & Tupper. He was a highly respected corporate lawyer and Dean of the Faculty of Law at UBC, but he did little court work.

On the other hand, he was well-liked, capable, efficient and forceful. Reggie Tupper was born in Ottawa and lived in Victoria and Vancouver before being sent off to the Royal Naval College at Osborne, England at the tender age of 12. He completed his midshipman's training and spent six years with the Royal Navy, but a bout of rheumatic fever quickly put an end to his naval aspirations. He returned to Vancouver and studied law.

above: 2810 Southwest Marine Drive (demolished).
PHOTO COURTESY JULIA TUPPER

left: Reggie Tupper with Julia, ca. 1958.
PHOTO COURTESY JULIA TUPPER

Tupper interrupted his studies to head back overseas and fight in World War I. He was seriously injured fairly early in the war and developed a morphine addiction, which he later kicked. He finished his studies and joined his father at the law firm. Like his grandfather and father before him, Tupper tried out politics and ran as the Conservative candidate for North Vancouver in the 1940 federal election. After he failed to win the seat he never bothered with politics again.

Hugh C. Murray, who entered the law firm in 1955, described Tupper as a real gentleman. "He was the kind of lawyer who went to the heart of the matter right away," Murray told law firm biographer Reginald Roy. "Mr. Tupper was the first lawyer to come to the office in the morning, usually by 7:30 a.m. at the latest."

Other colleagues described him as industrious, prompt and brusque, with a quick mind and photographic memory.

"Patience wasn't my father's ruling virtue," his son David told Roy. While another partner said: "I remember coming into his office and I'd say 'good morning,' and I would feel I had said at least one word too many. He was that precise."

By the time he retired in 1972, Tupper had spent 53 years at the law firm, and had at one point practiced alongside his son David.

Julia Tupper, David Tupper's daughter, says her grandfather was a quiet man who loved to read, garden and build in stone. She remembers visiting her grandparents at the Southwest Marine Drive house. "It was a huge piece of property and the house was a beautiful old English Tudor style, with a carriage house and a tennis court," she said.

Julia says he built a huge stone wall around the front of the property along Marine Drive. "My grandfather spent most of the years he lived there building this rock wall because he just loved rocks," she said.

In the 1930s Tupper built a house on Hermit Island—the island he bought a half share of in the 1920s and eventually owned outright. "Hermit Island was his great love," she said. "My father and his brother Gordie helped my grandfather bring 72,000 cobbles up from the beach and they counted every one of them."

Through all his years of practicing law, Tupper had remained relatively unknown outside of the legal community. That all changed in 1955, when he became a one-man commission into allegations of graft and corruption in the Vancouver Police Force.

Given Tupper's prompt and obsessively punctual nature, it must have driven him mad when Len Cuthbert's attempted suicide delayed the hearings by two weeks.

LEN CUTHBERT (1901–1986)
186 West 23rd Avenue

When the 54-year-old Cuthbert finally took the stand it was to a standing-room only crowd. Accompanied by his nurse, a visibly agitated Cuthbert stunned the court and spectators by admitting that he and Mulligan had split large sums of money over a three-and-a-half month period in 1949 when he was head of the gambling squad.

He counted off the amounts and the dates that he had accepted bribes on his fingers and named the gamblers who gave him the money. Cuthbert said that both he and Mulligan were doubling their salaries, helped by Joe Celona who was reportedly paying $200 a month in bribes.

Tupper's description of Cuthbert was less than flattering. Cuthbert, he said in his report, "had not the appearance nor does he give the impression of the hard villain who could or would plot the destruction of any person. He seems to be a man without strong moral fibre, and of an emotional disposition, upon whom others could exert an influence without great difficulty."

Detective Sergeant Len Cuthbert testified that bribes helped him and his boss Chief Mulligan double their salaries (1955) VPL 42995

Certainly Cuthbert had a seedy history within the police force since joining in 1926. Before Mulligan promoted him to detective sergeant, he had been disciplined and busted down in rank twice. The first time was for hanging out with criminals and supplying bootleg liquor to colleagues, and then in 1945 the police force suspended him for trying to seduce a woman in a case he was investigating. Mulligan, according to Cuthbert's testimony, had given him commendations over the years to help him climb back up in rank.

Cuthbert's private life would have put him under additional scrutiny. Cuthbert was married twice—the first time in 1934 to Marjorie Summers, a 19-year-old cashier who was 14 years his junior, and then in 1937 to Dorothy Smith, a 23-year-old nurse. In 1955, the year of the enquiry, they had an 18-month-old-son and two adopted daughters aged 12 and 16. At the time of his self-inflicted wounds he was described as "frightened, extremely agitated and extremely worried."

He certainly had reason to be.

Cuthbert told the hearing that he would meet Pete Wallace, an east side bookie, at the CNR Station near Main Street. Wallace would hand Cuthbert a paper bag containing $500 and two bottles of whisky. Cuthbert would keep the booze and hand over all the money to Mulligan, who would divide it in half and hand the rest back to be split among Cuthbert and the other cops on the take.

In 1942 Cuthbert paid Rosina Cappello, then a 62-year-old bootlegger, $4,000 for her house at 327 East 18th. Tupper looked into the transaction at the Inquiry but discounted it in the end as not being pertinent to his investigation.

Cuthbert said that he fell in with the chief's proposal because he wanted a promotion and was in need of extra money. And he was confident Mulligan would protect him. Cuthbert told Tupper that he was little better than broke in 1945 and then received an inheritance from his mother and scraped by until 1949, by which time he had burned through the money.

Cuthbert estimates his total haul was $1,150. He said he stopped taking bribes when he moved to the Dry Squad, because he felt he had no protection.

Cuthbert lived at the West 23rd address from 1940 to his death in 1987 from a combination of heart attack and emphysema. He lived to the ripe old age of 86.

left: Len Cuthbert bought bootlegger Rosina Cappello's East 18th Avenue house. EVE LAZARUS PHOTO

below: Walter Mulligan upgraded to this west side house in 1948. EVE LAZARUS PHOTO

WALTER MULLIGAN (1904–1987)
1155 West 50th Avenue

In 1928, Walter Mulligan was a year on the job and pounding a beat on Broadway between Granville and Main. While he was untouched by the police corruption scandal resulting from the Lennie Commission, it would have served as an interesting introduction to the culture of the Vancouver Police Department and underworld characters such as Joe Celona, Shue Moy and French Pete.

Mulligan made detective after 10 years on the job and had a fairly average career until 1943. In that year there was a messy hold-up at a blind pig on Howe Street and a man was killed. Mulligan solved the case and was promoted to superintendent

of the Criminal Investigation Bureau. The Liverpool-born son of a police officer hurtled over the heads of a dozen angry senior men, and by 1947 had the attention of Mayor Gerry McGeer.

That year, Mulligan went to the newly elected Mayor and told him of finding places "running wide open" and talked of "token raids" where police would go into a brothel or a bootlegging establishment and arrest an employee while leaving the proprietor alone. Mulligan charged that there was no determined effort to stamp out bootlegging, and told McGeer that: "My firm conviction is that these places could not operate without police knowledge and sanction."

McGeer agreed. He kicked out Chief Constable A.G. McNeill, along with the deputy chief, two inspectors, and 15 detectives. After the purge, 43-year-old Mulligan became the youngest chief constable in the city's history.

Mulligan had a commanding presence. Six-foot-two and 230 pounds, he was tough, seasoned, confident and always impeccably dressed. He married Violet in 1928 and they moved into a plain stucco house at 1166 East 16th Avenue. The couple never had children, and Mulligan, in sharp contrast to his muscular tough guy persona, was a gardener in his spare time and won prizes in local competitions for his flowers.

By 1955, Mulligan had 700 people under his command. He'd made a number of enemies and people were talking once again about police corruption and pointing their finger at the top cop. But if Mulligan was taking bribes in a significant way, it didn't show in his possessions. Just after he became chief, he and Violet moved to the house on West 50th. The plain weatherboard bungalow on a corner lot, while slightly more middle class, was certainly no palace. It was nothing like the grand houses of either McGeer or Celona, nor was it as pleasant as Ray Munro's North Vancouver cottage. Mulligan said he loved sailing, but he never had a boat. The only thing he seemed to spend money on was his mistress, Helen Douglas.

Mulligan did rent an apartment on the fourth floor of the newly built 1890 Haro Street, around 1955, but appears he never moved in. Reporter Ray Munro insinuated that it was a "love nest" for Douglas, but they'd been split up for years by that point and she had married someone else. On the other hand, it would have been impossible to keep both places just on his police salary.

Suite 401 at 1890 Haro St., Chief Mulligan's other home? (It's the upper floor under the penthouse, the two windows on the left)

Mulligan in pencil on the mailbox of the Haro St. haven.

According to Cuthbert's testimony, his involvement with Mulligan's profitable enterprise finished after three and a half months. It's not known how long Mulligan kept going or who with, as he never testified, and after his former lover took the stand, he left the hearing, grabbed his wife, and fled to the United States.

GERRY MCGEER (1888–1947)
4812 Belmont Avenue

By 1925, Gerry McGeer was a well established lawyer. He bought a large and opulent gated house on ritzy Belmont Avenue with a killer view for $25,000, and added a Stutz Bearcat—a black, long, low and sleek four-door car with windows made of shatterproof glass to his new garage.

A lawyer and later a Member of Parliament, Senator and Member of the Provincial Legislative Assembly, McGeer married Charl Spencer in 1917, daughter of Victoria's David Spencer, the department store owner. McGeer ran against L.D. Taylor for mayor in 1934 and won. On his first week on the job, McGeer oversaw the confiscation of a thousand slot machines, and he and his family spent most of the following year under heavy police guard.

McGeer lost the next election and continued his career in federal politics. In 1946 he ran again for mayor and won. He found the police force once again facing corruption charges.

Mulligan was the last major appointment McGeer would make before his fatal heart attack in August 1947. In a 1986 biography, *Mayor Gerry*, his daughter Pat recalls that the 59-year-old McGeer had come in to her bedroom at the Belmont Avenue house to say good night and talk about his recent trip. He reached for a large bottle of eau-de-cologne on her dresser and downed it in one swig. The next morning McGeer's chauffeur found him dressed in pajamas lying dead on the couch in his study.

left: Flash, June 25, 1955.

below: Gerry McGeer, 1932.
STUART THOMSON PHOTO. VPL 6636

RAY MUNRO (1921–1994)
550 Sutherland, North Vancouver

Ray Munro was good-looking, outrageous, arrogant and perhaps a touch insane. Jack Webster wrote about the first time he met him. He found Munro prancing around the *Vancouver Sun* room with a huge pair of shears, giggling and cutting other reporters' ties in half. Simma Holt, a former *Vancouver Sun* reporter, was in the newsroom one day when Munro marched in and cut the top off city editor Himie Koshevoy's fedora. "God he was a wild man," said Holt. "He was crazier than hell."

Munro's 1985 memoir *The Sky's No Limit* is full of his adventures as a fighter pilot in World War II, as a junior reporter at the *Toronto Daily Star*, and as a private pilot who flew a host of celebrities, including Robert Mitchum, Randolph Scott, Marilyn Monroe and Gary Cooper. He worked at the *Vancouver Sun*, at Artray—a company he co-founded with fellow photographer Art Jones of the *Province*—and then at *Flash*. Much later, after he moved away from Vancouver, he earned a living as a stunt pilot, as a touring hypnotist called "the Great Raymond," and as a motivational speaker lecturing executives on how to overcome fear.

Ray Munro's North Vancouver house.
EVE LAZARUS PHOTO

He once crossed the Irish Sea in a balloon during a raging storm; he taught parachuting to the US military in 1962, and in 1969 Munro made his 528th parachute jump onto a small ice floe in the North Pole.

While he gave his exploits a lot of ink in his memoir, Munro's two wives and five children got short shrift. After his first wife (the mother of Joanne and Rob) died from tuberculosis at 22, Munro left the children with his parents and took off to Mexico, where he wrote in great detail about meeting Errol Flynn. From Mexico he travelled to Vancouver and landed a job at the *Vancouver Sun* as a staff pilot and aerial photographer, and shortly afterwards, moved his parents and children first to White Rock, then to the house on Sutherland in North Vancouver.

Bernie Smith, a Vancouver policeman, remembered helping Munro find a call girl once for a story he was working on. Smith and Munro came to know each other quite well.

"When Ray Munro walked into a room it lit up like a Christmas tree," said Smith. "He had an absolutely dynamic personality. He was very good looking."

Bernie said Munro drove him home once and came into his house and told Smith's young daughter a story. "He took her photo right at the punch line," he said.

"You know White Rock [the landmark after which the suburb was named] was all painted black once? He's the guy who did it," said Smith.

Ron Rose was a *Vancouver Sun* reporter when Munro joined the paper in 1947. Rose has less than fond memories of Munro. "Ray was a guy that was good to stay away from," said Rose. "He was a loose cannon from the beginning."

On one occasion Munro and Art Jones stole an ambulance, said Rose. On another, Munro took his young son Rob up in a plane, fastening him in with safety pins. Rose says he never flew with Munro: "I wouldn't even drive with the guy!"

In the 1940s the *Vancouver Sun* was in the Sun Tower on West Pender Street. Rose says Munro, Jones and the other photographers used to have a lair right up in the top of the building, under the dome, where they'd go for a drink.

When Munro broke the police corruption story in *Flash*, Rose says rather than be awed by his investigative skills, most of the media were just annoyed at him. "We figured he was rabble-rousing and it was probably not true," said Rose. "The *Sun* wasn't anxious to jump on it in case it was libelous."

Simma Holt feels that Munro took advantage of police confidences. "A lot of the police were victims of Munro," she said. "He'd sit down in the snake room and they'd talk freely in front of him. He had the trust of all of them and then he turned on them."

Holt was a reporter on the police beat at the time and remembers once scooping Munro on a story at the police station. "He grabbed my knee and he almost broke it, he was so strong. He was so angry that I had scooped him."

Ray Munro, ex-detective Jack Whelan, Chief Walter Mulligan, Constable Stan Leacock and others at the police probe, 1955.
BILL DENNETT PHOTO,
VANCOUVER SUN 24258196

Tupper's report of February 17, 1956 certainly dismissed a lot of Munro's stories. Tupper didn't believe Jack Whelan's story that he and Mulligan once stole a piggy bank when they were partnered as detectives, neither did he find Munro credible.

"I do not think it unjust to conclude that Munro thinks of the world in terms more suitable to a melodrama than to the usual, though sometimes tragic, circumstances of everyday life," Tupper wrote in his report. "I think he is unable to dispense with sensationalism and has found in times of peace that it arises most easily in exposing the wrongs of others."

2915 West 29th Avenue.
EVE LAZARUS PHOTO

The Tupper Commission ran from June 1955 to January 1956, saw 126 people testify—everyone from petty gamblers to the Attorney General, a former mayor, and a judge. Some of the most sensational testimony came from Bob Leatherdale, a highly respected second-generation policeman.

ROBERT WILLIAM LEATHERDALE (1905–1986)
2915 West 29th Avenue

Shortly after Bob Leatherdale was promoted to detective sergeant in 1949, he was approached by Mulligan, who asked him if he was interested in heading up the liquor squad. Leatherdale was definitely interested, but balked when he found out that there were major strings attached.

Leatherdale told the Tupper Commission that Mulligan sent Cuthbert to his house to discuss the appointment. As head of the liquor squad, Cuthbert told him, it would be his job to "put pressure" on those bootleggers who weren't paying for protection. The idea, he was told, was to drive business to bootleggers who were paying—and then named half a dozen of these known bootleggers including Blondie Wallace, Jack Craig, a "Mrs. Emily," and Joe Celona. Leatherdale would then be expected to pick up the pay-off money from them and take it to Chief Mulligan, who would give him back half to divide among himself and his men.

"There is no use beating about the bush, we might as well talk straight," Cuthbert told him. "The chief wants money."

Cuthbert told him that he and the chief were doubling their annual salaries of $5,000 and $10,000 respectively.

"It would have been my job to collect monthly and to split with the chief and the men of the liquor detail," Leatherdale told the inquiry. Cuthbert told him that Celona was paying $200 a month and that this would soon rise to $300 if business picked up.

"My personal opinion of the chief was that until 1949 I thought him absolutely on the up and up," Leatherdale said under cross examination. "I changed my mind."

Leatherdale turned down the job and went to prosecutor Gordon Scott, Magistrate Oscar Orr and Mayor Charles Thompson with the details of these conversations.

Some weeks later Scott told him that he had spent time and money looking into the allegations against Mulligan, but he couldn't find any direct evidence to confirm that he was taking bribes.

Leatherdale gave his notes to Detective Sergeant Archie Plummer, who after confirming them with Cuthbert, took them to Scott.

Scott told Plummer that his allegations could be construed as jealousy of Mulligan, and once again nothing was done.

Helen Douglas in disguise with Mrs. Lefeaux at the police probe, 1955. VPL 42996

HELEN ELIZABETH DOUGLAS
3910 East Georgia Street, Burnaby

Up until the testimony by Helen Douglas, the only thing missing from the Tupper Inquiry was sex. Mulligan's former mistress testified that he paid for trips to the Okanagan, Vancouver Island, Montreal and Seattle. She said Mulligan gave her a diamond ring, two large pieces of unset jade, a zircon ring, a Chinese teak chest and a typewriter. A *Province* headline of 1955 screamed: "Woman said Mulligan gave her $2,200 for love nest" in Langley.

Mulligan's mystery mistress came to court flanked by her lawyer and his wife, Mrs. Lefeaux. She wore a blonde wig, heavy rimmed glasses and a large brimmed blue hat all wrapped up in a veil to confound the waiting photographers. The veil came off in court, but everything else stayed hidden including her new married name and the identity of the man she married in 1953.

Douglas testified that she met Mulligan, at the time a detective, at the Quadra Club in 1944 while she was celebrating her 30th birthday. They were together for five years, and split when Mulligan refused to leave his wife, Violet, to marry her.

Two of her neighbours were questioned as witnesses, and they described seeing Mulligan arrive at different times of the day and night, sometimes on foot, sometimes in a police car and sometimes driving a 1936 Plymouth. William Abbott said he'd seen Mulligan visiting Douglas twice a week over a period of years, while William Mitchell, who lived across the road, gave the titillating piece of information that he saw Mulligan arrive one evening and not appear again until 8:00 a.m. the next morning, when he saw Douglas kissing him wearing only her robe and her hair braided down the sides. Tame today, but scandalous back in the 1950s.

The Whelan's bought the East 17th Avenue house in 1930.
EVE LAZARUS PHOTO

Douglas acknowledged that she was a reluctant witness, only coming forward because police were harassing her friends and family. She was cagey in her testimony, but admitted knowing that Mulligan was married.

When Tupper asked if Mulligan was receiving any money, she answered that it was her impression that he might have been.

"I guess there was some money being paid out, but I don't know to whom. It was his business, not mine," she said.

Of the $2,200 Mulligan gave her in cash for the Langley property, Douglas said it was to be bought in her name to have for him. Her answers were carefully guarded. "I had the impression that it wasn't his salary."

Financially, Douglas was doing quite well on her own. Her adopted mother had left her some money and she already owned a couple of rental properties in the city. In 1952, Mulligan told her to sell the Langley property and keep the money for herself. The property deed described her as the wife of Walter Hugh Douglas—no such person existed.

What caused the reporters to run to the phones was Douglas's admission that Mulligan had told her he had $38,000 in cash received from gamblers hidden in a safe place. And she said that Mulligan had mentioned a plan to her that divided the city into two sections—east and west—each of which would be controlled by a big-time gambler who would pay for police protection.

Immediately after Douglas left the box, Mulligan's lawyer announced that his client would be leaving the hearings and was ready to face trial on whatever charges would be laid.

HARRY WHELAN
1325 East 17th Avenue

Harry Whelan, uniform division superintendent, was the truly great tragedy to come out of the hearing. Unlike his brother Jack, a dodgy ex-cop and bodyguard for Munro, Harry Whelan was a well-respected, honest cop.

Whelan testified that as Mulligan's deputy chief, he refused to take money from gamblers and it cost him a demotion to superintendent. Whelan also had a sad personal life story that he desperately wanted to stay private, and he was told a lot of his family history would come out under cross-examination.

Three hours before taking the stand for a second time, the 53-year-old Whelan took his .38 revolver and shot himself in the chest at his home. He died in the same room, using the same gun that his father had used to kill himself years before. According to reports at the time, and to Bernie Smith who worked for Whelan, the shooting had nothing to do with police bribes, but was because he was afraid that personal information about his father, and his daughter who had also committed suicide, would come out at trial and embarrass his wife and two young sons.

THE AFTERMATH

The outcome of the Tupper Inquiry was an anti-climax. On the last day in January 1956, Tupper found that, with the exception of Cuthbert and Mulligan, he couldn't be sure of anyone else's guilt. And, while he gave the police commission, the prosecutor, and the mayor a good verbal spanking, the Attorney General ruled that there wasn't enough evidence to support Tupper's finding of corruption and could not take the case to court.

above: Harry Whelan, 1951 Vancouver Police Department portrait.
VANCOUVER SUN PHOTO 24076590

below: Crowd spilling into the police probe, 1955. VPL 43921X

At the time of his dismissal, Mulligan had become the longest serving police chief in Vancouver's history, and perhaps because he held so much promise, one of the worst. He fled south of the border, worked at a California nursery, and then later as a limo/bus dispatcher before returning with the loyal Violet to Oak Bay in Victoria to retire. He died there in 1987 at age 83.

Out of all the people involved in the Mulligan Affair, only Cuthbert lost his job. He was fired, not for taking bribes, but because his suicide attempt was against police regulations. He managed to get work as a security guard for Lenkurt Electric Co., and by 1970 had worked his way up to security supervisor.

As for Ray Munro, he had a brief stint as the editor of the *Chatham Daily News* in Ontario, then left the newspaper business altogether. He was awarded the Order of Canada in 1975 for his assistance in establishing the Canadian Aviation Hall of Fame, and he died of cancer in 1994, survived by four of his five children.

Out of all his career choices and projects, one of his most lasting legacies is the collection of photographs he took when he briefly partnered up with fellow *Sun* photographer Art Jones in their company Artray.

CHAPTER 7

A Century of Entertainment

For the last century, Vancouver has supplied Hollywood with some of its most interesting actors and entertainers. London-born William Henry Pratt arrived in 1910, sold real estate, married here, divorced here and built a piece of the Pacific National Exhibition before becoming Boris Karloff in 1913. His 1931 movie portrayal of Frankenstein's monster made him a household name.

Vancouver born Peggy Yvonne Middleton followed a similarly bizarre trajectory. She was enrolled at June Roper's Dance School, danced at the glitzy Palomar Supper Club, and lived with her grandparents in a huge white frame house on Comox Street in the West End before becoming Yvonne de Carlo. At her peak she was one of Hollywood's leading sex symbols, starring in dozens of movies and as Lily Munster—who was married to the Frankenstein-esque Herman Munster—in the 1960s television sitcom *The Munsters.*

In 1922 (the year de Carlo was born), a West End girl named Sadie Marks met Jack Benny while he was performing his comedy act at the Orpheum. Apparently she heckled him from the front row. Five years later, they married and moved to Los Angeles and she became radio celebrity Mary Livingstone.

4 East 51st Avenue

When Martin and Jennifer Butler bought their house in 1993 they had no idea that the modest East Vancouver home was once the headquarters for a thriving Vancouver theatre company. The

left: Bryan Adams outside the Marine Building.
ROBERT KARPA PHOTO, ©1989

below: The headquarters of a thriving theatre company in 1930.
PHOTO COURTESY OF MARTIN AND JENNIFER BUTLER

previous owners had lived in the house for half a century, and things were largely unchanged. When the Butlers started to renovate the basement they found that the walls were insulated with over 30 hand-painted theatre posters featuring The British Guild Players—a professional repertory company that performed at the Empress Theatre during the 1920s and '30s.

Married actor couple Dorothy Hammerton Clyde and David Clyde had performed on the stage, first in Scotland and then in England, as part of the Garrick Theatre Players. The Clydes moved to the United States and performed in Boston and on Broadway between 1925 and 1928. The following year they partnered up with playwright and actor Norman Cannon, moved to Vancouver, bought and refurbished the Empress Theatre and launched the British Guild Players.

"Their productions were usually light-hearted 'forget the Depression' comedies with titles like *Bunty Pulls the Strings* and seasonal pantomimes such as *Peter Pan* and *Rip Vancouver Winkle*," says Martin Butler. "We also found advertising posters for the candies sold at intermission."

Dorothy paid $2,700 for the East 51st house in 1930. The house became the business and artistic headquarters for the Clydes, hosting stars of the time such as Fanny Brice, Dorothy Somerset and Basil Rathbone.

When the Butlers renovated their house they found posters and an old Rogers Golden Syrup can filled with British condoms behind the walls.
PHOTOS COURTESY OF MARTIN AND JENNIFER BUTLER

Dorothy owned the house until 1938, but the couple had already moved to Hollywood where they were establishing quite a movie career for themselves. Dorothy became film star Fay Holden, and appeared in 46 films between 1935 and 1958, but was best known for her role as Mickey Rooney's mother in the Andy Hardy movies. David—the brother of Andy Clyde of Hopalong Cassidy fame—found steady work as a character actor in a variety of movies, including the *Philadelphia Story* (1940), *Jane Eyre* (1943) and *The Scarlet Claw* (1944).

The Butlers are at a loss to explain why these highly regarded actors landed in Vancouver instead of going straight to Hollywood, but they say the good vibes of the Clydes have left their mark, because the house is directly across the road from Langara College's Studio 58. As well as discovering the Clydes, their ongoing renovation has turned up live ammunition, an old Rogers Golden Syrup can filled with "British Throughout" wartime condoms, and a 1928 postcard from a young girl studying at the University of Washington that says: "Seattle is a bum place, why didn't you come and see me off? Love, Fanny."

The house, Martin Butler says, remains "an ongoing story."

opposite top: Demonstrators from the Post Office and Art Gallery sit-in marching in front of the Empress Theatre, 1938 (demolished). VPL 1293

opposite bottom: Ivan Ackery and Marilyn Monroe at the premiere of *Gentlemen Prefer Blondes*, July 1953. VPL 59307

THE EMPRESS THEATRE (1908–1940)
276 East Hastings Street

By 1913, Vancouver had eight movie theatres as well as stock theatres like the Empress and the Pantages. And while other theatres were modified to accommodate motion pictures, the 1,650-seat Empress was used exclusively for live acts.

In his book *Fifty Years on Theatre Row*, theatre Manager Ivan Ackery wrote about lavish productions that called for sheep and horses on stage, as well as cars. For

Faust, he wrote, the stage crew built fire-breathing dragons 20 feet long; for *The Aviatrix* they constructed a copy of the new Wright Brothers aeroplane and flew it on piano wire.

Ackery notes that the Clydes' British Guild Players achieved a whole new level of polish and sophistication that kept stock theatre going in Vancouver long after it had died out almost everywhere else except New York.

In the late 1930s, rising costs, talking movies, and the shift of the city away from Main Street sounded the death knell for the old theatre and it was torn down in 1940.

Ackery was there when the Empress was demolished. One of the workmen showed him a powder puff that he had found beneath a floorboard. The name "Pavlova" could still be seen on its handle. Anna Pavlova—the great Russian ballerina—danced at the Empress in 1910.

In 1933, the year that David Clyde sold his half-share in the Empress, a *Vancouver Sun* article noted that between the stagehands, electricians, designers and actors, the theatre had a payroll of $1,500 a week, which qualified it as a significant employer in Vancouver.

IVAN ACKERY (1899–1989)
6951 Isleview, West Vancouver

During the more than three decades that Ivan Ackery managed the Orpheum Theatre he became almost as famous as the celebrities he hosted. Among the show business legends that he met were Marilyn Monroe, Susan Hayward, Ella Fitzgerald, Louis Armstrong and Duke Ellington.

Ackery used to hang out with Gary Cooper when he was in town, often stopping at one of the local bootleggers where they once joined Mayor Fred Hume to exchange "philosophies of life and all those profound things one discusses in an afternoon at the bootleggers," he wrote in his memoir.

Ackery started his theatre career as an usher soon after World War I. By 1930, he was managing the Dominion Theatre on Granville, and in 1932 he was transferred to Victoria to manage the Capitol Theatre. When a bylaw banned Sunday movies, he brought in monthly midnight movies on Sundays. Famous Players obviously liked his initiative because they brought him back to Vancouver to run the much larger Strand Theatre, and in 1935 he was promoted to the Orpheum where he managed a staff of sixty-five.

Radio and the Great Depression were taking their toll on theatre and Ackery needed to use all his skill at promotion to create the magic that would bring the crowds back.

Chuck Davis recalled that Ackery was known as Mr. Orpheum, Atomic Ack and Little Orpheum Ackery. He won two awards for his promotions, which Davis noted was the equivalent of an Oscar. Ackery once paraded a cow down Granville Street that wore a sign saying: "There's a great show at the Orpheum and that's no bull."

In those days Ackery and his assistant managers wore tuxedos to complement the luxurious surroundings, gold leaf, and silk tapestries that would help to transport patrons from their often all-too-serious lives. Usherettes were used to being dressed up in the movie theme of the moment—whether that was as pirates or cowboys. Occasionally the theatre hired local First Nations people to be dressed and on hand for western movies.

For some performers, Ackery's Alley would have been their only view of Vancouver.
EVE LAZARUS PHOTO

Ackery pulled off one of his biggest coups when he landed the February 1940 Canadian movie premiere for *Gone with the Wind*. Vivien Leigh's daughter attended a private school in Vancouver and was in the audience (but incognito, at her mother's insistence). Stars often came to town for their premieres. When Susan Hayward attended the 1942 world premiere of *The Forest Rangers*, she sprained her ankle, and Ackery happily picked her up and carried her onto the stage.

In 1954, he moved from his West End apartment at 1144 Haro and paid a dancer named Delmar $4,800 for half an acre in Copper Cove, just near Horseshoe Bay. Ackery built a house on the lot and lived there for the next 20 years. "I wasn't a gardener, but I did the same as I'd done in show business, just learned as I went along, and in time the property became a very beautifully landscaped one," he wrote. "I built a rockery, with stairs, right down to the water, and planted it all myself . . . It became so attractive and so popular, that the sightseeing buses used to bring people to see it."

Ackery managed the Orpheum from 1935 until his forced retirement at age 70 in 1969.

While there is a star outside the theatre on Granville Street with his name on it, in 1985 Mayor Mike Harcourt proclaimed October 30th as Ivan Ackery Day and presented Ackery with a plaque naming the alley behind the theatre in his honour. Ackery's Alley is a typically dirty downtown alley, but at one time limos dropped off the stars at the door to the Orpheum, and to the Commodore Theatre a few dumpsters down. It was also the route which whisked them back to their hotels or on to nightclubs like the Penthouse or the Cave. For some, rushing from performance to performance in city after city, Ackery's Alley would have been their only view of Vancouver.

Four years after Ackery retired, he was back working to save the much loved Orpheum from turning into a multiplex cinema for Famous Players and following other great theatres, such as the Capitol, the Strand and a Pantages, into oblivion.

THE ORPHEUM THEATRE
884 Granville Street

When the "new" Orpheum was built in 1927 for $1.25 million it was one of the biggest theatres in Canada. The Orpheum was designed by B. Marcus Priteca, a Seattle-based architect who designed nearly 200 theatres over the course of his career, including 22 for Alexander Pantages, an impresario who at the height of his career owned 84 theatres in North America. The theatre owner liked the way the architect worked a budget, and once told Priteca that "any damn fool can make a place look like a million dollars by spending a million dollars, but it's not everybody who can do the same thing with half a million."

Priteca fashioned the theatre in a Spanish renaissance style and gave it an opulent air with some sleight of hand tricks of his own. For instance, the theatre's ornate ceiling is made of plaster and chicken wire, which hides the real, much plainer ceiling above. He introduced a range of different influences including Italian-inspired terrazzo floors and travertine walls, crests of British heraldry, Czechoslovakian crystal chandeliers and Baroque ceiling and dome covers.

Priteca was able to shave more money off the cost by siting the main entrance on Granville Street, but building the auditorium on Seymour, where land and taxes were cheaper. He connected the auditorium to the entrance by a walkway over the alley.

When Famous Players decided to demolish the Orpheum in 1973, they were completely unprepared for the outrage that this generated—possibly the biggest heritage protest in Vancouver's history. City Hall received 8,000 letters from angry citizens and petitions with 1,000 signatures. Ackery bounced back from retirement and joined impresario Hugh Pickett to stage a benefit concert starring Jack Benny.

The City of Vancouver bought the Orpheum for $3.9 million and poured another $3.2 million into a renovation by Thompson, Berwick, Pratt architects. The theatre is now the permanent home of the Vancouver Symphony Orchestra.

Looking north on Granville Street ca. 1946 as Lady Luck plays at the Orpheum. CVA 1184-2305

In 1965, King Rat, a World War II story about a Prison of War camp starring George Segal, had its Canadian premiere at the Orpheum Theatre. James Clavell, the Australian-born author who wrote the book the movie was based on, was in attendance. As were a number of POW's who lived around the Vancouver area whom Ackery had been able to locate. In typical Ackery style, he set up a big dinner and press conference at the Georgia Hotel before the premiere.

James Clavell wrote *Taipan* from his West Vancouver house in 1962.
EVE LAZARUS PHOTOS

JAMES CLAVELL (1924–1994)
7165 Cliff Road, West Vancouver

Although James Clavell is known for epic best-selling novels such as *Shogun*, *Noble House* and *Gai-Jin*, he was actually a screenwriter and director who got his start writing the screenplay for *The Fly*, a 1958 movie starring Vincent Price. He also wrote the screenplay and directed the wildly successful *To Sir with Love* starring Sidney Poitier, and the 1963 *The Great Escape* starring Steve McQueen.

At his wife April's suggestion, Clavell wrote his first novel, *King Rat*, during a screenwriter's strike in 1960 and based it on his experiences as a prisoner of war at the Changi camp in Singapore during the Second World War.

"About 150,000 of us got captured and of those, 10,000 walked out—one in 15. Most died of malnutrition, the majority working on the Burma railroad," he told *Vancouver Sun* reporter John Armstrong a year before his death. "Nobody'd told me I couldn't write a book, so I did, and it certainly saved my marbles because it was a form of catharsis. I wrote it in about six to eight weeks and it had a lot of purple prose so it had to be heavily rewritten, but it got rid of all the hate I'd stored up and released me from penury."

In 1962 Clavell used the $200,000 advance he got for *King Rat* to buy a house perched on a cliff in West Vancouver's Whytecliffe neighbourhood, quite near to Ackery. He wrote his second novel *Tai-Pan* from one of the seven bedrooms that looks out onto Howe Sound.

Jan and Mike Volker have owned the house since the mid-1990s. Jan points to the living room ceiling and says the first owner was Remette Davis, a concert pianist who had an acoustic ceiling so she could broadcast for the CBC from her home. The Clavell's were the second owners, but only stayed for a few weeks at a time, mainly using the residence as a summer home and break from Los Angeles. Clavell wrote, produced and directed *The Sweet and the Bitter*, a 1967 movie that looked at the horrible treatment of Japanese-Canadians during the Second World War, while living in the West Vancouver home. The movie was the first and only movie produced by

Commonwealth Film Productions, an early attempt to establish a viable film industry in Vancouver, and was shot at a West Vancouver studio and at various locations around the city including the BC Hydro Building (now called the Electra).

The movie went over budget, eventually premiered at the Orpheum in 1967, and was a complete flop. In *Dreaming in the Rain*, Peter Prior, a construction worker on the set of *The Sweet and the Bitter* told author David Spaner that Clavell was known for having all work grind to a halt in the afternoon. "He used to have to have a silver tea service on a silver tray every afternoon. We used to think it was quite amusing," said Prior.

Clavell and April and their two daughters Holly and Michella lived in West Vancouver until 1972. They moved to Switzerland and the house sold to Gary Troll, owner of Troll's restaurant in Horseshoe Bay. Troll won $14 million in the lottery in 1997.

In 1986 Clavell broke literary records when he received a $5 million advance for his novel *Whirlwind*.

Errol Flynn aboard the *Zaca*.

ERROL FLYNN (1909–1959)

Clavell wasn't the only Australian-born celebrity to make an impact on Vancouver. More than half a century has passed, and locals still talk of Errol Flynn's spectacular death.

Flynn, 50, was pronounced dead at Vancouver General Hospital on October 14, 1959 with Beverly Aadland, his 17-year-old girlfriend, at his side. The next day Vancouver was plastered on the front page of newspapers all around the world.

Officially, Flynn's death was from "Myocardial Infarction, coronary thrombosis, coronary atherosclerosis, fatty degeneration of liver, portal cirrhosis of the liver," but in unscientific language, Flynn lived life like one of the movie characters he played and his fatal heart attack was helped along by booze, drugs, three divorces, two statutory rape trials, and a bevy of young starlets.

Flynn, whose star had faded some years before, was in Vancouver to sell his luxury yacht the *Zaca*, one of the last assets he still owned. But while jaded and broke, he was still remembered as a Hollywood legend swashbuckling his way out of Tasmania and onto stardom in more than 60 movies, including *Captain Blood*, *They Died With Their Boots On*, and *The Adventures of Robin Hood*.

Flynn and Beverly, a child actor who had appeared in one of his movies two years before, arrived on October 8 and overstayed their welcome with George Caldough, a stock pro-

above: The West End apartment building where Errol Flynn died in 1959.
EVE LAZARUS PHOTO

right: Errol Flynn's autopsy was performed by Glen McDonald at the East Cordova Street morgue. His official cause of death was myocardial infarction, coronary thrombosis, coronary atherosclerosis, fatty degeneration of liver, portal cirrhosis of the liver.

moter Flynn knew who said he could broker the sale of Flynn's yacht. From all appearances Caldough and his wife were living the good life in a luxury house on Eyremont in West Vancouver's British Properties. What people didn't know was that the house was rented, the Caldoughs were nearly broke, and a few years later Caldough was to end up in jail at the wrong end of a stock scam.

Perhaps Flynn was looking at other options, because at one point he met with George O'Brien Junior, who was interested in buying the *Zaca*. Former Royal Vancouver Yacht Club historian Jock Ferrie was at the Vancouver Lawn Tennis Club that day and was chatting to O'Brien when Flynn and Beverly turned up for lunch.

"Here is Errol Flynn at the door, and they won't let him in because he's in bare feet, doesn't have anything on his chest, and he's clutching a bottle of Wolfschmidt Vodka in each hand," recalls Ferrie. "The club secretary came to us and said we don't know what to do with Mr. Flynn, and George said 'don't worry, I'll kit him out.'"

Ferrie said that O'Brien was an extremely respected, well educated and wealthy member of the RVYC who burned through three fortunes in his lifetime. He also owned four yachts, including *Mir,* which he kept in California. So at least financially, outfitting Flynn in the Vancouver Lawn's pro shop with appropriate club attire wouldn't have been a problem.

A few days later the Caldoughs were driving their guests to the airport when Flynn started complaining of severe pain in his back and legs. The most credible story is that Caldough knew Dr. Grant Gould and took Flynn to his West End apartment at 1310 Burnaby Street. What's not clear is why and how a bunch of other people turned up to meet him there. At one point he was supposedly standing up against a wall to relieve the pain in his back, telling stories of his exploits with other Hollywood celebrities, and the next moment he excused himself, said he needed to lie down for an hour, and—presumably forgetting his flight and empty bank account—that he would then take everybody out for dinner. He went into Dr. Gould's bedroom, lay down on the floor and died.

Ferrie doesn't know what happened to the deal with O'Brien, whether the price was too high, or if Flynn died before it could be concluded, but O'Brien did not buy the *Zaca*. Instead the luxury yacht, built for wealthy San Francisco railroad heir Templeton Crocker in 1929, and that had once transported Orson Welles and Rita Hayworth in the filming of *The Lady from Shanghai*, was stripped, sold off and left to rot. In 1979 newspapers reported that the current owner had an exorcism to "drive the ghost of Errol Flynn from his yacht" and brought her back to her former glory.

At the time of writing, the *Zaca* was berthed in Monte Carlo.

MICHAEL J. FOX (1961–)
7150 Fulton Avenue, Burnaby

Michael J. Fox was born in Edmonton two years after Errol Flynn's death and would go on to give Vancouver a completely different kind of fame.

The son of an army officer, Fox spent his early childhood living on military bases from Chilliwack to North Bay, Ontario. When William Fox retired from the army in 1968, he and wife Phyllis and their five children moved into a three-bedroom apartment in Burnaby.

The apartment building was across the street from a sprawling strip mall with a parking lot that easily accommodated street hockey. That parking lot was likely the inspiration for Michael's first career choice of professional hockey player.

Fox's grandmother was a huge influence in his early life, and lived just a block and a half away in a blue three-storey apartment building.

William Fox took a post-retirement job as a dispatcher for the Ladner police. Phyllis worked as a payroll clerk in a cold storage plant on the waterfront, where, at 15, Fox spent the summer making coffee, filing and running errands. He spent his $600 earnings on a 1967 wood-grained Fender Telecaster guitar.

Michael J. Fox at the 1988 Emmy Awards. PHOTO ©1988 ALAN LIGHT

"As I saw it, rock and roll offered a far more realistic shot at the big time than the NHL," Fox wrote in *Lucky Man*. "Of course to everyone else in my working-class Canadian world…both fantasies were equally ridiculous."

In the summer of 1977 Fox was in an acting troupe at Burnaby Central Secondary School when his drama teacher Ross Jones told him about a casting call for a new CBC series called *Leo and Me*. Fox won the role of the 12-year-old Leo and earned a whopping $6,000 that summer. He continued to get small parts on television shows, in radio and ads, and in 1979 left school and took a road trip with his father to Los Angeles.

What's more impressive than his amazing career—starring roles in *Family Ties*, the *Back to the Future* trilogy, *Spin City* and *The Michael J. Fox Show*, is how he's handled Parkinson's, the disease he was diagnosed with in 1991. He and wife Tracy Pollan have raised four kids, Fox has continued to act, and in 2011 he was awarded the Order of Canada for his outreach and fundraising work through the Foundation he created in 2010.

While Fox was making his mark on Hollywood, Vancouver was producing a number of rock stars who were making an international impact on music.

93

DOUG BENNETT (1951–2004)
2146 Semlin Drive

Doug Bennett was born in Toronto, moved to Vancouver in 1973 and became a graphic artist at the *Georgia Straight*. Four years later he formed Doug and the Slugs, and by the early 1980s he was on top of the music world. Doug and the Slugs notched up four gold albums, and toured across the country. Bennett emerged as a respected singer and songwriter, actor, producer, video maker and comedian. He even designed his own album covers.

above: Doug Bennett once described his stage performance as "Neil Diamond on acid."

right: Doug and the Slugs ca. 1980
HANS SIPMA PHOTOS

below: Rumour has it that Doug and the Slugs once painted a mural of the history of Canada on the dining room wall of the Bennett's Semlin Drive house.
EVE LAZARUS PHOTO

The band, whose stage performance Bennett once said was "like Neil Diamond on acid," had several hits that Bennett wrote, including "Making it Work" and "Tomcat Prowl."

When he couldn't get bookings, Bennett promoted his own dances, and when record companies rejected his songs, he launched his own label. "Too Bad" became a top-10 hit in Canada.

Vancouver Sun reporter John Mackie described him as an "improbable rock star."

"In an age of glamorous video-friendly performers, Bennett was an Everyman in a Sally Ann Suit, an independent spirit who succeeded through sheer determination and a unique talent," Mackie wrote.

Bennett released his solo album *Animato* in 1986 and a year later he and his wife Nancy and their three daughters Della, Shea and Devon moved into a large house in Vancouver's Grandview area. The Bennetts lived in the 1911 Craftsman for over a decade.

The house was built by Charles Kilpin, a carpenter and builder who sited the house on the brow of the hill on a corner lot. He filled it with large art glass windows, fireplaces and lots of verandahs. Kilpin lived there with his family until 1920, when the house sold to Harry Wilson and his wife Susie. Harry owned Wilson's Shoe Store and the house stayed in the family for the next half-century. Other families followed, until the Bennetts bought in 1987. One story has it that the band used to practice in the house, and painted a mural on the dining room wall of their perspective of the history of Canada.

Bennett died in October 2004, just a few weeks shy of his 53rd birthday. At the time of his death he was on tour in Calgary, had separated from his wife and was living at the Eldorado Motor Hotel on Kingsway. Bennett's cause of death was never revealed, just that he had died from causes related to a "long-standing illness."

BRYAN ADAMS (1959–)
100 Powell Street – Warehouse studio

Like Michael J. Fox, Bryan Adams was a military brat born in Kingston, Ontario. His parents split in 1973 and his mother Jane brought Bryan and his brother Bruce to live in North Vancouver. Local legend has Adams attending almost every school in the Lower Mainland, but he did live in Lynn Valley for a short time and spent brief periods at Argyle and Sutherland Secondary before quitting school at age 16.

Adams performed in local bands such as Shock and Sweeney Todd, and in 1983 released his third album *Cuts Like a Knife,* which quickly soared up the charts and established him as a rock star and probably the Canadian musician with the most name recognition outside Canada.

Along the way Adams has collected a ton of hardware and accolades, including 20 Junos, a Grammy, an Oscar, the Order of British Columbia, the Order of Canada for contributions to music and philanthropy, and in 1998, a City of Vancouver Heritage Award for transforming a derelict Gastown warehouse into a world-class recording studio.

When Adams bought the brick building at the corner of Powell and Columbia Streets in 1991, it was abandoned and abused. Likely it would have gone the way of other historical Gastown buildings if he hadn't seen its potential.

"When I bought the place, it was a burnt-out shell with vagrants living in it for shelter," Adams told Bob Clearmountain in a 2000 interview for *Mix.* "But I saw the potential instantly. Since then, the area has sprouted all kinds of restaurants and mad cafes."

The Victorian-style warehouse is the oldest brick building in the city. Built by David Oppenheimer, a German immigrant and Vancouver's second Mayor (1888-1891), the building was partially built in 1886 and its cellar survived the Great Fire that year. It then housed the Oppenheimer Brother's growing wholesale grocery business. The warehouse was also Vancouver's first City Hall while Oppenheimer was mayor.

The building restoration took seven years and cost $5 million including the purchase price. The three-storey building has large windows to let in lots of natural

above: Bryan Adams transformed a derelict Gastown warehouse into a world-class recording studio.
EVE LAZARUS PHOTO

below: Recording Studio
BRYAN ADAMS PHOTO

Michael and Brandee Bublé,
ca. 1982.

light, a massive main studio on the second floor and a mixing suite on the third floor. There are two lounges for bands to unwind in and Adams also bought the adjoining building at 102 Powell, gutted it, and put in a small parking lot with a basketball hoop and a two-hole golf putting green.

"I always leaned toward having a studio in an eccentric neighbourhood," Adams told *Mix*. "It reminds me a little of New York."

Others who appear to love the historic studio include AC/DC, Elton John, Bon Jovi, The Tragically Hip, Metallica and Michael Bublé.

MICHAEL BUBLÉ (1975–)

Michael Bublé dreamed of becoming a singer and an entertainer from the time he was five years old. In *Onstage, Offstage* he writes that his career kicked off when his father taught him to sing the family's address for the house where he grew up in Burnaby. "That little song was my first foray into music, and it came to me as naturally as shooting a hockey puck," wrote Bublé.

When his parents, Lewis and Amber Bublé, bought him Bryan Adams' *Reckless* he knew that if Adams, another local boy, could have so much success, then so could he. "To know that this guy had done it was really inspirational," Bublé told ABC News in 2007.

A more important influence in Bublé's life is his grandfather Mitch Santaga, a plumber who was born in Alberta in 1927, moved to Union Street when he was one year old, and lived in Strathcona until 1954 when he married and moved to Burnaby.

"He was the biggest supporter a young man could ever have," says Lewis Bublé. "When Michael would sing in malls or shopping centres, Grandpa would go with him, sipping coffee endlessly while he waited."

Santaga says his grandson had a natural talent.

"I couldn't believe it was him singing. Michael would sing his songs and we were all excited we thought he was tremendous back then," he said. "He's always been a

good boy," says Santaga. "He's very generous and he tries to help people out all the time. I'm proud of him."

Bublé and his two younger sisters Crystal and Brandee went to Cariboo Hill Secondary. Bublé spent every summer working with his father, a commercial fisherman, until he won the Canadian Youth Talent Search in 1995.

Santaga shrugs off his own involvement with his grandson's early career, though Bublé has often told interviewers that his grandfather got him hooked on music by listening to jazz greats like Ella Fitzgerald, Mel Torme and the Mills Brothers. Santaga also paid for his music lessons.

In an interview with ABC News, Bublé said his grandfather would say: "If you let him get up and sing, I'll put in a free toilet for you."

Santaga jokes that he only installed "a couple" of toilets before his grandson's career took off.

"My grandpa will sit in the studio for hours while I record, and he'll fly halfway around the world to watch me perform—even though he's in his eighties," wrote Bublé in 2011.

Bublé got his big break in 2000 when he was singing "Mack the Knife" at the wedding of Caroline Mulroney, daughter of former Prime Minister Brian Mulroney. He caught the attention of David Foster, who was a guest at the wedding, and who would produce many of the albums that went on to earn Bublé three Grammy Awards, multiple Junos and a worldwide audience.

Like Michael J. Fox, another Burnaby native, Bublé had dreamed of being a hockey player, and while that particular career path didn't pan out, in 2008 he became a part owner of the Vancouver Giants.

Bublé married Luisana Lopilato, an Argentinean actress and model in 2011, and their son Noah was born two years later at North Vancouver's Lions Gate Hospital.

Lewis and Amber Bublé still live in their Burnaby home, and the family remains tight. "I think whacko would describe us better," says Lewis Bublé.

top: Michael Bublé in concert.
PHOTO ©2014 PHIL KING

bottom: The Bublé's Burnaby home.
EVE LAZARUS PHOTO

CHAPTER 8

Legendary Women

"Never retract, never explain, never apologize—get the thing done and let them howl!"
--Nellie McClung, 1915.

NELLIE YIP QUONG (1882–1949)
783 East Pender Street

Wayne Avery knew nothing about the history of his house until one day he found an elderly Chinese woman peering through his front room window.

He invited her inside and discovered that she was Eleanor (Yip) Lum, and that she had been born in his Strathcona house in 1928 by Nellie Yip Quong, who later adopted her.

Nellie was not Chinese, as her name suggests, but a white Roman Catholic, born Nellie Towers in Saint John, New Brunswick and educated in the United States. It was while she was teaching English in New York City that she met and fell in love with Charles Yip, a successful jeweller from Vancouver. Charles was the nephew of Yip Sang, a wealthy merchant who built the Wing Sang Building on East Pender in 1889. The building was erected to house Yip Sang's growing import/export operation, an opium production plant, and his family.

When Nellie and Charles married in 1900, it was the first interracial marriage in Vancouver. After they were married, Nellie was disowned by her family and spurned by the church. The couple decided to leave Canada and lived in China for a few years. They moved back to Vancouver in 1904.

The young couple moved in with Yip Sang at 51 East Pender, now the oldest building in Chinatown and the renovated offices of Bob Rennie, Vancouver's "condo king." Rennie has installed an art gallery at the back of the building where Yip Sang once housed his three wives and their 23 children—one wife per floor. Rennie also retained the Chinese schoolroom where Yip Sang's progeny learned Chinese. It was in this room where Nellie mastered a remarkable five different Chinese dialects and learned how to communicate with the Chinese and with the authorities who ignored them.

left: Tosca Trasolini, 1939.
PHOTO COURTESY ANGELA STEPHENS

below: Eleanor (Yip) Lum in front of the East Pender Street where she was born in 1928.
PHOTO COURTESY STARLET LUM

Nellie fought on behalf of the Chinese. She challenged the justice system and shamed the Vancouver General Hospital into moving non-white patients out of the basement. When the White Lunch restaurant put up a sign saying "No Indians, Chinese or dogs allowed," Nellie made them take it down. She arranged care for the elderly, brokered adoptions, acted as an interpreter, and became the first public health nurse hired by the Chinese Benevolent Association.

Nellie and Charles moved into their East Pender Street house six blocks away in 1917.

Nine decades later, Wayne took Eleanor through the house where she had grown up. He toured her through his newly renovated home, room by room. She'd stop here and there and point out something from her past—the bedroom, where Nellie helped deliver an estimated 500 Chinese babies, the dining room where Nellie had played Mahjong, and the rooms where the kids that she and Charles fostered stayed. Eleanor told Wayne that Charles did the cooking and the gardening, and one of her favourite memories of Nellie—a large imposing woman—was her wearing a wide hat with a feather in the side and reading a Chinese newspaper on the bus.

During the renovation, Wayne had discovered that at different times his house was once a bootlegging joint and a brothel. He found old Finnish newspapers beneath the floor, cartons of cigarettes stashed in the ceiling, booze in a secret hideout in the garden, and locks on the inside of the bedroom doors. After Wayne found out about Nellie, he started doing more sleuthing. He found that in 1911 Nora and Ross Hendrix, grandparents of rock star Jimi Hendrix, lived in his home.

According to Engineers Canada, female enrolment in engineering programs in Canada peaked at 20% in 2001 and now hovers around 18%. It's almost impossible to imagine how determined a young woman must have been to earn a degree in the male-dominated field of engineering in the 1920s. Yet that's exactly what Elsie MacGill did. And then she did much more.

ELSIE GREGORY MACGILL (1905–1980)
1492 Harwood Street

Elsie MacGill grew up in Vancouver's West End in the early years of the twentieth century. While other little girls in her dance class dreamed of performing on the stage, Elsie was more interested in finding out how things worked. As she grew older she was interested in how things flew. In most households these ambitions would have been knocked out by high school, but Elsie had what other girls could not imagine—a mother who believed that anything was possible and had proved it over and over again.

Born in 1864 to a wealthy family in Hamilton, Ontario, Helen Gregory wanted to be a concert pianist. But she didn't just want to take lessons, she wanted a university degree. It took some pull from her grandfather the judge, but Helen was allowed to study at Toronto's elite Trinity College. She made history when she became the first woman to graduate with a Bachelor of Arts degree. When she was 26, Helen spoke to the Canadian Club in Washington. Reporters dubbed the small pretty anomaly the "Pocket Venus," but her solid grasp of international affairs impressed *Cosmopolitan*'s editor (the magazine wasn't always about orgasms) and he offered her a job as a foreign correspondent travelling throughout Japan and China.

Helen's first husband was a doctor named Lee Flesher. She supported him financially through medical school, and moved with him to Minnesota. When he died just a couple of years into their marriage, she raised their two small boys.

A few years later, Helen reconnected with James MacGill, an old flame from college who was a sometime prosperous lawyer, writer and real estate speculator in Vancouver. She married him, had two more children, and her interests turned to the law and fighting for the rights of women and children.

In 1908 the MacGills moved into their big new mustard-coloured house on Harwood Street. The house had a billiard room in the basement and out back, chickens and a kitchen garden which Lee Wa Kee, "the Chinese help," cultivated. It was a privileged existence for Elsie and her older sister Helen. The third floor of the house was converted into a classroom when the girls were too young to attend Lord Roberts Elementary on Bidwell.

Helen and Elsie took art lessons from a struggling Emily Carr, who rented a studio on West Broadway in 1912. The girls learned to swim in nearby English Bay under the watchful eye of volunteer lifeguard and local legend Joe Fortes. Friends of their mother's who visited the house included the famous suffragettes Nellie McClung and Helena Gutteridge.

The house is still there, one of the few that managed to withstand the apartment blitz of the 1960s. It's now a strata conversion painted a regal red. At the side you can see a weird pattern of bricks on the outside fireplace. The bricks, says the current owner, came from the Great Fire of 1886.

opposite: Nellie Yip Quong spoke five Chinese dialects and helped deliver around 500 Chinese babies.
PHOTOS COURTESY STARLET LUM.

above: The MacGills moved into what was in 1908 a new mustard coloured house.
EVE LAZARUS PHOTO

below: Elsie MacGill, 22.
COLLECTION OF RICHARD BOURGEOIS-DOYLE

When the economy tanked in 1913 so did the MacGill's fortunes. By 1915 they were forced to sell the Harwood Street house and move to rented digs on Haro Street.

Helen's law career was far more successful than James'. When BC led the country by establishing a minimum wage board, she was the only woman on its first board. In 1917 she became the first woman judge in BC presiding over Vancouver's Juvenile Court.

Nearly a decade later, she could afford to buy back the Harwood Street house, and in 1927 the MacGills were able to host their eldest daughter Helen's wedding to Everett Cherrington Hughes, a professor of sociology, at the family home.

Elsie, now 22, returned home for her sister's wedding. After getting booted out of UBC's engineering program for being female, Elsie found acceptance at the University of Toronto. In 1929, when she became the first woman to graduate from the program, she contracted polio. Elsie was told that she'd never walk again and she returned home to the Harwood Street house to spend the next few years fighting through intense pain. It didn't stop her dreams of designing airplanes, and when she was accepted into graduate studies in aeronautical engineering at MIT she returned to the east.

The firsts didn't stop. Like her mother, Elsie went on to challenge the traditional roles of women and played a leading role in the war effort. She was the first woman aircraft designer in the world, the first female member of the Association of Professional Engineers of Ontario, and at the outbreak of the Second World War, this tiny formidable woman, bent over on her crutches, ran the Canadian Car and Foundry in what is now known as Thunder Bay. As chief engineer, Elsie converted an old railway car plant into a facility with over 4,500 employees and churned out three Hawker Hurricane fighter planes a day. The Hurricanes were crucial to the

In 1942, Elsie became known to millions of little Americans through a comic book as the "Queen of the Hurricanes" for her work on the Hawker Hurricane fighters.

Battle of Britain, and by the end of the war CanCar had built 2,000 Hurricanes —one out of every 10 that were ever produced.

Elsie was 38 when she married Bill Soulsby and started a consultancy business in Toronto. She kept her own name and once told a reporter: "I never go under the name of Soulsby. Even my husband calls me Miss MacGill. Actresses and writers have that privilege, so should engineers."

In 1967 Prime Minister Lester Pearson named her as one of seven commissioners on the newly established Royal Commission on the Status of Women, where, like her mother, she fought for women's equality. In 1971 she was made a member of the Order of Canada. York University awarded her an honorary doctorate of science in 1978, and after her death from a car accident at 75, she was inducted posthumously into the Engineering Hall of Fame and Canada's Aviation Hall of Fame.

Because of her partial paralysis Elsie could never fly a plane, but she insisted on being a passenger on all test flights, saying that this was the only way she could properly assess an aircraft's performance. And even before she designed her first plane, she argued in an article she wrote for *Chatelaine* that physical strength had nothing to do with flying a plane. All it took was a few pounds of pressure to move the stick, the rudder and work the pedals.

top: Helen's wedding in August 1927. Elsie far right.
COLLECTION OF RICHARD BOURGEOIS-DOYLE

Bottom: Tosca Trasolini in 1936 proving that a woman's place is in the air.
PHOTO COURTESY ANGELA STEPHENS

Tosca Trasolini proved that Elsie MacGill was right. The young woman stood less than 5'2" and proved to be a superb athlete, motorcyclist and pilot.

TOSCA TRASOLINI (1911–1991)
850 East 12th Avenue

It was a cold drizzly November morning in 1936 when 25-year-old Tosca Trasolini climbed into the cockpit of a Fairchild bi-plane, secured her helmet, adjusted her flying goggles, rolled the bi-plane down the runway and disappeared into the fog. As one of the Flying Seven, Canada's first all-female aviators' club, she was the first to fly in the dawn-to-dusk patrol.

The seven women took turns flying over Vancouver in 25-minute stints in two Fairchilds, a Golden Eagle, two Fleets, and two Gypsy Moths. They were trying to make a point, they said, that a woman's place was in the air.

Six of the Flying Seven ca. 1940 (Tosca Trasolini second from right).
CVA 371-987

Besides Tosca, the club included Margaret (Fane) Rutledge, Rolie Moore, Jean Pike, Betsy Flaherty, Alma Gilbert, and Elianne Roberge. Fane and Roberge held their commercial pilots' license.

The club had formed in 1935 after Margaret Fane flew to California to meet with Amelia Earhart, president of the Ninety-Nines—an American organization for women pilots. There weren't enough experienced Canadian pilots to form a chapter, so the Canadian women started their own. The newspapers of the time called them the "Sweethearts of the Air," "flying flappers" and "angels," defying what a *Chatelaine* article had asked a few years earlier: "Are women strong enough to fly with safety? Are they fitted temperamentally to operate aircraft?"

The idea for the dawn-to-dusk protest began after the seven women attended an airshow sponsored by the Vancouver Junior Board of Trade, and were told they couldn't go onto the field to examine the aircraft.

"Can you imagine it?" Tosca told the *Vancouver Sun*'s Stuart Keate. "We were just as interested in the different machines as a lot of men around the place, but they stopped us at the gate. Told us we couldn't go in. But don't worry, we made it. I had to get hold of a little ribbon allowing you admittance, but I got inside. I looked over all the aeroplanes and then passed the ribbon out to the other six girls outside and they came in one by one."

The Trasolini family house on East 12th.
EVE LAZARUS PHOTO

Tosca told Keate that she'd always wanted to fly. "I had always been crazy to do it. I just didn't have enough money to follow it up, until I got this job," she said, referring to her job as a stenographer for Angelo Branca's law firm. Branca had also grown up in Strathcona at 343 Prior Street, a few blocks from the Trasolini's.

Tosca worked as Branca's legal secretary for over 20 years. The *Canadian Lawyer* magazine rated him as the most famous criminal defense lawyer in Canadian history.

The Trasolini family was well known in Strathcona, living at different addresses on the 400-block Union Street before moving to East 12th around 1918.

Norman was a fireman, a star baseball player for the Vancouver Mounties, and a scout for the St. Louis Cardinals. During the war he served as a captain in the Canadian forces. His brothers Elmo and Salvador also served, as did their sister Fulvia, who was a sergeant in the Women's Army Corps assigned to US Army Intelligence. Fulvia married an American sailor after the war, had a baby daughter Angela, and settled in California.

Tosca tried to enlist in the Canadian Air Force, but she and the other six members of the Flying Seven were swiftly rejected. They were women, after all.

Rather than remain grounded, these women used their remarkable skills and determination to contribute to the war effort.

The Flying Seven sponsored the first aerial training centre for women in Canada, they taught flying theory and parachute-packing and sent out their grads to work at Boeing's Seattle plant and in aircraft factories in eastern Canada—quite likely at Elsie MacGill's CanCar plant.

In 1940, they borrowed a couple of planes and staged a raid from Vancouver to New Westminster. This was what they called a "bomphlet," dropping 100,000 flyers with messages such as "dimes or dollars to buy our boys more planes," and "Smash the Nazis." They raised enough funds to pay for eight planes for the flight training school in Vancouver.

Tosca moved to Los Angeles in 1949. Her niece Angela says that correspondence she has between her aunt and Branca indicate that they had a "close personal relationship." Angela's mother told her that Tosca was "run out of Vancouver," and family speculation was that knowledge of their relationship might come out when he was vetted for a judiciary appointment. Perhaps it did, because he was not appointed to the Supreme Court until 1963.

Angela says her aunt drove a red convertible, flew a Cessna, and joined the flying club at the nearby airport at Compton.

When Angela, a tennis player, admired Tosca's diamond ring, her aunt said she could have it if she won a national championship. Angela won, and still has the ring, along with a number of her aunt's pictures, records and a set of Minton Buckingham china dishes that she had received as a present when she was briefly engaged to be married in Vancouver in the 1930s.

In 1961, at age 50, Tosca married Leland H. Tenhoff, a career military officer. The marriage lasted seven years and Angela believes marriage just didn't suit her aunt's temperament.

After her divorce Tosca bought 10 acres of land and built herself an 800-square-foot cabin at Adelanto in the California desert.

"There were no utilities, she had to truck in her own water," says Angela. "Her neighbour was also a pilot and they had a landing strip there and they used to fly in and out."

The Trasolini family ca. 1940s. (Tosca Trasolini far right).
PHOTO COURTESY ANGELA STEPHENS

Bottom: Phyllis Munday at the Alpine Blaeberry Camp, ca. 1950s.
PHOTO COURTESY DEBORAH MUNDAY

Tosca didn't just smash ceilings to become one of the country's first female aviators, she was also a natural athlete, busting records in track and field, baseball, basketball and lacrosse. She held the women's discus record for British Columbia in the 1930s.

Legend has it that she once humiliated all the young men in the tight-knit Vancouver Italian community when she was the only one who could shinny up a greased pole to collect the cash at the top.

While Tosca Trasolini flew over the tops of mountains, it was Phyllis Munday who conquered them.

PHYLLIS JAMES MUNDAY (1894–1990)
373 Tempe Crescent, North Vancouver

"My love for the mountains is terribly deep," Phyllis Munday wrote in her diary. *"They mean so much. It is impossible to explain what they do to your soul. There is nothing on earth like them."*

A reporter once asked Phyllis Munday if she'd ever been really frightened during all her years of climbing mountains. "Thunderstorms," she told him. "I hated thunderstorms."

What she didn't mention was the time she saved her husband Don Munday's life from a grizzly bear by charging at it with an ice axe; when she regularly carted 60 pounds of backpack over flood-swollen creeks; the times she had to avoid quicksand and avalanches and hidden crevasses.

"It was just something you had to do to get to the mountain," she once said. "Once you got above the line it was beautiful."

In 1955, Phyllis Munday accompanied Sir Edmund Hillary, of Mt. Everest fame, on a helicopter tour of BC's coastal mountains. Three decades before that she and Don had headed up the expedition that led to the discovery of Mount Waddington, the highest peak in the province at 13,176 feet. The Mundays called it Mystery Mountain.

Back in the 1920s, the BC coastal mountains were a vast, unknown and virtually unmapped area. The Mundays attempted to conquer Mount Waddington three times, and although they never reached the summit, Munday's skills as a scientist, cartographer and adventurer opened up the area for others.

Mrs. Munday brings her third load of sixty pounds across Scar Creek.
Photo A.R.Munday.

Deborah Munday says that not reaching the top of Mount Waddington was something that her aunt always regretted. "It was important to her," says Deborah. "When they filmed this show called *Thrill of a Lifetime*, they took her to the glacier near Mount Waddington and when she came down she said 'if I could die I would die up there, that's where I wanted to be.'"

Phyllis Munday thought nothing of crossing swollen creeks carrying 60 pounds on her back.
PHOTO COURTESY DEBORAH MUNDAY

Born in Ceylon—Phyl's father managed Lipton's tea estates—the James family moved to Vancouver when she was 13. Every chance she got, Phyl would travel to the North Shore mountains, and in 1912 she led her Girl Guides troop to the top of Grouse Mountain. In 1983 she told Chuck Davis that "Going up Grouse Mountain, I thought I'd conquered the world."

She met Don Munday, a writer and a wounded soldier who served at Vimy and who was a patient at the hospital where she worked. She quickly discovered that they shared a love of mountains, and married him in 1920.

Two hours after their 9:00 a.m. wedding they were in their climbing gear and trekking up one of the local mountains. The birth of Edith the following year didn't slow them down at all; they simply strapped her to Don's back and kept on climbing.

Mountaineering expedition in 1926.
IMAGE 1987-04-001 ROYAL BC MUSEUM
BC ARCHIVES

The Mundays lived first in a tent on Grouse Mountain and later in a cabin, thinking nothing of scrambling up and down the mountain whenever they needed supplies or to attend meetings. When Edith turned six in 1927, they bought a small frame house on Tempe Crescent.

It wasn't exactly on a mountain top, but it was close.

right: The Mundays bought the Tempe Crescent house for the view in 1927.
EVE LAZARUS PHOTO

below: In November 2012, friends and former students of Valerie Jerome dedicated a bench in her honour next to her brother Harry's statue in Stanley Park.
PHOTO COURTESY VALERIE JEROME

"We bought it for the view," Phyl once said. "It was such a blow to come off the mountain, we thought that at least here we'd have some of the same marvellous outlook. We see all of Vancouver spread before our feet, and over to Vancouver Island, I can see Mount Arrowsmith. To the west, Horseshoe Bay, the Lions, and the Tantalus Range way in the distance."

Don died in 1950 and Phyl lived in the house for the next four decades, surrounded by photographs that she had taken of her mountains.

When Phyl was 93, she moved from her house to Nanaimo to live with Deborah's mother and father. She took her two favourite possessions—a chair that she always sat in, and a framed photograph of Mt. Robson, the highest mountain in the Canadian Rockies.

Deborah says that her aunt thought of Mt. Robson as "her" mountain. In 1924, Phyl was the first woman to reach its summit. She and Don scaled over 100 peaks together and clocked up other firsts. They were the first to ascend Mt. Coquitlam and Golden Ears. In the 1930s, they were the first to explore the Klinaklini glacier fields. BC's Mount Munday, only a few kilometres southeast of Mount Waddington, is named after them.

Phyl was commemorated with a postage stamp in 1998 and received an honorary doctorate in law from the University of Victoria. Shortly after she received the Order of Canada in 1973, she told a reporter: "I haven't a clue why they gave me the Canada medal. I must admit it surprised me because there must be hundreds of people far more worthy than I."

Most people have heard of Harry Jerome. His name adorns recreation centres and his statue is in Stanley Park. At one time he was the fastest man alive, setting a total of seven world records. In 1970 he was made an officer of the Order of Canada. Fewer people remember his sister Valerie, yet she is just as amazing.

VALERIE JEROME (1944–)
704 East 17th Avenue, North Vancouver
Valerie Jerome had just turned 7 when she moved with her family from Winnipeg to North Vancouver. Along with her sister Carolyn, 10, and brothers Harry, 11 and Barton, 6, they moved in across the road from Ridgeway Elementary. Valerie still vividly remembers her first day at that school.

"We didn't even get onto the road. It seemed like every kid in the school was lined up with rocks," she said. "I can still remember the feeling of the first rock that hit my back as we ran."

Valerie doesn't like to think much about those days, but every February, for more than a decade, she drove across the bridge from Vancouver, returned to her old elementary school and talked to the kids about those early days for Black History month.

She started by pointing to the house at 416 Lyon Place where they lived, and where in 1953, fire broke out during the middle of the night when the sawdust burner caught fire. Valerie was sent to ask a neighbour to call the fire department, not because she was the oldest—she wasn't—but because she was the whitest. The family were left out on the street while the neighbours watched from behind their curtains.

"Nobody came out to help us. My mother was pregnant with my youngest sister and we finally got a cab to the Salvation Army Hall on Lonsdale," she said. "The family spent the night on chairs."

In 1954, the Jeromes bought a small rancher on East 17th, near their next school, Sutherland Junior Secondary. Valerie opted to work in the school cafeteria at lunch time, rather than sit alone at a table or go home.

The year she turned 15, everything changed. In that year Valerie became one of the fastest women alive. She set Canadian records at the 1959 Canadian Track and Field National Championships in her running events, broke her age group record for long jump, and helped her team win the relay. She won bronze at the Pan-American Games in Chicago, and the following year, she joined her brother Harry to represent Canada at the Summer Olympics in Rome.

The media of the day called them the "dusky brother and sister athletes."

"All these people who had been spitting at us and calling us niggers every day of our lives were there," she says. "Then I went to North Vancouver High after I had been to the Olympics and I was invited to eat with everybody. That's what is called a whitewash—you have a little bit of celebrity and somehow our brown skins turned white."

The City of North Vancouver held a dance in their honour and gave them $500 each to spend.

Sport, she says, made everything bearable. "When the stopwatch gave you a great time, it didn't matter what colour you were."

Unfortunately, things at home were deteriorating rapidly. Their father, a railway porter, was away for days at a time. Carolyn moved to Winnipeg and Harry took a scholarship at the University of Oregon. Barton, who was mentally challenged, had been shipped off to Woodlands School years before, and Valerie was left at

top: The Jeromes house on Lyon Place, North Vancouver. EVE LAZARUS PHOTO

above: In 1954, the Jeromes bought a small rancher on East 17th Avenue. EVE LAZARUS PHOTO

home with her youngest sister Louise to take the brunt of her mother's physical and verbal abuse.

When she was 16, she ran away from home and went to live with a foster family in South Burnaby.

Once when she came home to pick up some clothes she found that her mother had emptied hundreds of family photos and news clippings about her and Harry on top of a refuse heap in the backyard and set them on fire. On the top was a photograph of her grandfather, John Armstrong "Army" Howard, who competed for Canada in the 1912 Summer Olympics. He was wearing Olympic shorts and T-shirt in the picture.

"When I went to pick it up, it just crumbled in my fingers," she says.

Harry Jerome died from a brain aneurysm in 1982. He was 42, and Valerie never really recovered from his death. It was because of her sheer determination that Stanley Park now has a statue of her brother. Over the years she has worked to keep his name alive and celebrate his achievements on and off the track.

At the same time, Valerie has quietly made a huge impact. She went to university, became a teacher and taught in Vancouver for 35 years. She spent three decades as a track and field official. Between the mid-1980s and 2000, Valerie ran in eight elections for the Green Party, federally, provincially and civically.

"I did not do that with any expectation of being elected, but it was a way of getting green ideas out there. Nobody was talking about the environment at all in those days," she said. "We were talking about recycling, of a car-free downtown, and looking at global warming and ozone depletion issues." Her son, Stuart Parker, led the BC Green Party from 1993 to 2000.

Valerie says she keeps in touch with hundreds of her former students, and on November 10, 2012 many of them came to Stanley Park to see a bench dedicated in her honour.

The bench is a fitting tribute. It simply reads: "Valerie Jerome. Canadian Olympian. Celebrating her career as an athlete, teacher, coach, community activist. This bench is dedicated to her, here beside her brother Harry."

above: Harry and Valerie Jerome at the airport, 1966.
PHOTO COURTESY SFU
SPECIAL COLLECTIONS

right: Joy Kogawa.
PHOTO COURTESY GORDON KOGAWA

JOY KOGAWA (1935–)
1450 West 64th Avenue

Joy Kogawa's childhood house is a modest wood-framed bungalow in South Vancouver. There's really nothing architecturally significant about it, except that it's one of the few original houses that remain in the neighbourhood. What makes the house of great historical importance and worth preserving is its social history.

The house, which was built in 1912, figures prominently in Joy's classic novel *Obasan*, written in 1981 and named one of the most important books in Canadian history by the Literary Review of Canada. The book was adapted into a children's book called *Naomi's Road* and then into a 45-minute opera that toured elementary schools in British Columbia.

"It was my little Paradise Lost," says Joy. "It was a place of togetherness and I remember it very well."

The house is a physical reminder of the time when 22,000 Japanese-Canadians—fishermen, miners, merchants, and foresters—were wrenched from their homes, sent off by train to the Interior and interned during the Second World War. Joy's father was a clergyman at a church in Kitsilano and Joy and her brother Timothy Nakayama were only small children when they were taken from the family home and sent to an internment camp in Slocan, BC.

The house, which they'd owned since 1937, was auctioned off at a bargain price by the government's Custodian of Enemy Alien Property.

It was a shocking period in Canada's history. The house is an important monument to that time. "This little house is just a tiny, tiny echo of something much more unthinkable," she says.

Obasan tells the story of the Japanese internment through the eyes of six-year-old Naomi Nakane, who, in 1942, had her family ripped apart by the war.

"The house, if I must remember it today, was large and beautiful," Joy wrote in *Obasan*. "I looked it up once in the November 1941 inch-thick Vancouver telephone directory. I wrote to the people who lived there and asked if they would ever consider selling the house, but they never replied."

Joy goes on to write that the house she remembered had a hedge and rose bushes and flowers and cactus plants lining the sidewalk. The backyard had a sandbox and an apple tree and a swing, where she would dangle by her knees.

Looking back to that time, Joy says when they were taken away from their home she missed her dolls, her books, music and people who were always coming and going. "To me the house was very sumptuous because we had rugs and soft couches and running water and electricity," she said. "All these things that make a child's life rich."

The family moved to Alberta after the war and Joy went on to study at the University of Alberta and the University of Saskatchewan. She was made a Member of the Order of Canada in 1986.

In 2003, Joy who now lives in Toronto, was visiting Vancouver and driving up Oak Street when she remembered the house. She was stunned to find that it was for sale for over $500,000.

Joy Kogawa's childhood home features prominently in her novel *Obasan*.

"I had dreamed so much of being able to buy it back one day," she said, "There were all these new houses, so I thought it was probably gone, and then I saw it and there were For Sale signs in the front." The asking price, she says, was impossible.

When it looked like the new owner was set to demolish the house, a group of writers and heritage die-hards formed the Joy Kogawa Homestead Committee and joined with The Land Conservancy to save the house from demolition. Currently, the house is on the City of Vancouver's Heritage Register with a B status and has a writers-in-residence program. The plan is to make it a historical literary landmark, and ideally it will be designated at some point to preserve it for the future.

"The house is doing very good work," says Joy. "It's there, it's survived, it remains as a place where a story has been told and it's part of our heritage. I think it's important for it to be kept, so many things get lost."

CHAPTER 9

House Murders

Grant Stuart Gardiner, a realtor who specializes in selling heritage houses, says that in all his years of selling real estate he's only ever been asked once if there had been a death in the house. He was showing a house on North Vancouver's Grand Boulevard when a woman came to look, but refused to go up the stairs. "She said there's some weird spirits or something spooky about this house." Much later a neighbour told him that a man had hanged himself in the attic back in the '50s.

left:
Helen, Dorothy and David Pauls.
COURTESY VANCOUVER POLICE MUSEUM

"If there has been a murder you are duty-bound to disclose it if asked, but there's no duty to research it and try and figure it out," he says.

Old houses have stories, but over the years they fade in people's memories. Murders that happened before newspapers went online are just not that easy to find. House numbers change, neighbours move away, people forget, and while some homeowners will serve up a murder as dinner party fodder, most live in fear that a murder will bring down the value of their home.

The murder stories that follow were pieced together from newspaper reports at the time and describe the most plausible scenarios based on those accounts. Back in those days, forensic science was limited and nobody but the murderer really knows what happened, or why these killings happened when they did.

On June 10, 1958, 52-year-old David Pauls was shot three times in the head with a .22-calibre revolver and beaten after he was dead. The killer then went upstairs and clubbed 11-year-old Dorothy Pauls to death in her bed. When Helen Pauls, 45, returned from work a short time later, the killer shot her twice in the head and then beat her dead body with a blunt instrument. It was Vancouver's first triple homicide.

THE PAULS MURDER

David Pauls glanced at his watch and saw that it was almost 11:30 p.m. and time to pick up Helen from the bus stop. It was raining hard outside, and he put on his

above: Helen's purse lies open on the kitchen table in this police crime scene photo.
COURTESY VANCOUVER POLICE MUSEUM

below: Neighbours watch on in another crime scene photo.
COURTESY VANCOUVER POLICE MUSEUM

hat, coat, and rubber overshoes for the short drive two blocks away. Dorothy, 11, had gone to bed hours before. He didn't disturb her.

Carrying his flashlight, David left the small stucco bungalow by the side door, as he always did, and headed for the old pickup truck. He was surprised to see a stranger approach him from his backyard, but surprise quickly turned to fear when he saw the gun. The man told him to go back inside, and when David hesitated, the stranger hit him with the butt of his gun. Confused and scared, David staggered back to unlock the door. The man put the gun to the back of David's head and pulled the trigger. The bullet from the .22 passed through the brim of David's hat, but didn't kill him. The man dragged him inside and down into the basement, and taking a lace from a pair of shoes, tied it around one of his wrists. As David regained consciousness, the man shot him in the head, then again in the left temple. And then even when he was sure he was dead, he began to beat him with the butt of his gun, breaking his skull in two places.

While the rain muffled the sound of the gunshots to the neighbours, the noise likely woke Dorothy. The little girl either yelled out to her father or the killer knew where her room was, because he made his way up the hallway to her bedroom. He saw her sitting up in bed surprised and scared, and smashed in her head with one savage blow. As she fell back, he finished beating her to death. He took the girl's robe and carefully wrapped it around her head. As he pulled off her pyjama bottoms, he heard the sound of running outside. He went to the bedroom window, knelt down, placed his palm against the wall and he saw Helen Pauls holding a

newspaper over her head and running to the front door. Helen let herself in, threw her purse on the kitchen table, and headed up the hallway to Dorothy's room. The killer stepped out and shot her in the face. The bullet travelled through the lens of her glasses and into her right eye. She fell to the floor and he shot her again in the side of her head. He then began to beat her. He left the same way he came. As he cut across the yard he dislodged a rock near the garage.

Missing from Work

When Helen failed to show up to work the next day, her worried colleagues called police. At 5:30 p.m. Constables Bob Engle and Russell Reid pulled up outside the Pauls' bungalow on East 53rd. The first thing they noticed was the advertising flyers on the porch. Reid, the junior partner with just two years on the job, pounded on the door. When no one answered he walked around the back. He found the porch door unlocked and he opened it and knocked on the inside door.

"I turned the knob and it opened and I can still tell you what I said: 'Ooohooo, is anybody home?'"

Reid noticed a woman's purse, open, with the contents spread across the kitchen table. He entered the hallway and saw Helen Pauls lying face down, shards of glass from her smashed glasses lying around her face, blood spread out in front of her and around her head. She was wearing a dress, short coat and shoes.

"I bent down and touched her leg. I probably shouldn't have, but I did and it was cold," says Reid. "I called to my partner—'Bob you should see what we've got here,' and he must have heard the quivering in my voice because he said 'let me in!' and I opened the door and he had his revolver out and we searched the house."

The horrified officers proceeded along the hallway. They found Dorothy's body on the bed, wearing only the top half of her pyjamas, with one leg stretched out to the floor. Her clothes were neatly laid out ready for the next day.

The officers walked down into the basement.

There was so much blood on the floor upstairs that it was dripping through the ceiling and onto the mat in the basement, said Reid. As they entered the basement the officers saw the fully-dressed body of David Pauls lying in a pool of congealed blood in the otherwise neat and tidy room.

Constable Reid said the murders haunted him for years. In those days there were no grief counselors and the 23-year-old officer was traumatized by the scene and plagued with nightmares.

The Pauls

Both David and Helen were of Dutch descent, born in Russia. David came to Canada in 1923, lived in Saskatchewan until 1940, and then spent eight years farming in Aldergrove before moving to Vancouver. People remembered the Pauls as hard working, frugal and having no enemies. When they moved to Vancouver, they first lived with friends at 5751 Sophia and soon after moved to 596 East 44th. The Pauls bought the house on East 53rd about 18 months before they were murdered.

Helen Pauls was shot and beaten to death in her Vancouver home. 1958 Police crime scene photo.
COURTESY VANCOUVER POLICE MUSEUM

below: The Pauls house on East 53rd Avenue (demolished 1971).
COURTESY VANCOUVER POLICE MUSEUM

At the time of the murders, David Pauls was a janitor with Woodwards, and Helen had worked at the Home Fancy Sausage Shop at 264 East Hastings Street for the previous three years. Dorothy went to Walter Moberly Elementary school.

On the day of the murder, Dorothy was the first home and practiced on the piano. Her friend Edel Friesen visited for a while, but left at 7:00 p.m. By 8:00 p.m. Dorothy was in her room doing homework. Helen worked the 3:00 to 11:00 p.m. shift, and after Evelyn Roche's murder she had become wary of walking home alone. She expected David to be waiting at the bus stop as he did every night, and would have been worried when he failed to show.

The Roche house on East 6th Avenue.
EVE LAZARUS PHOTO

EVELYN ROCHE

Even before the brutal murder of the Pauls family, people on the east side of town were on edge. Just three months earlier, Evelyn Roche, a 39-year-old wife and mother of two, was stabbed to death a short distance from her home on East 6th and Penticton Street.

A man from the neighbourhood found her body as he was on his way to work the night shift at the Canadian National Railway. Roche was lying on her back in the lane between 7th and 8th Avenues, dressed in a tan skirt, green blouse and sweater. It was cold out and she wore red gloves and a dark blue coat.

An autopsy determined that Roche was stabbed three times in the neck, twice in the right breast, and five times in the back. Each wound had been delivered with such force that the whole of the blade had entered her body. Her body had been dragged by the legs and her underwear was ripped and blood-smeared. There were blood stains around each ankle. Police found two brown paper bags about 30 feet from her body. One contained two pounds of grapes, the other a bottle of Canadian Club with a receipt from a liquor store on Pender Street.

When police went to her home they found her daughter Karen, 15, and son Frank, 14, who told them that their mother had caught a bus downtown around 8:00 p.m. to mail some parcels to their father, who worked for a logging company at Seymour Inlet. Police determined that she had arrived back a little over two hours later and was walking home when she was attacked outside the entrance to the lane. Her purse was found in a dumpster the next day still intact. While her clothes were ripped, there were no signs of sexual assault.

The fifth murder of that era that remains unsolved took place the following year.

LILA ANDERSON

On the morning of December 26, 1959, two 10-year-old boys were heading out to a nearby field to play with their new cap guns. Instead they discovered the naked body of Lila Anderson, 38.

Anderson had caught the bus home after having dinner with friends. She owned a house at 30 East 15th Avenue where she lived alone and rented out a section of the house to a married couple. She worked as a cashier at Safeway.

Instead of arriving safely, Anderson was murdered and dumped into a small ravine at Knight and 45th Avenue. The boys found her lying on her back, her right arm extended out. The only clothes she had on were silk stockings that hung around her ankles and a black skirt that the killer had wrapped around her head. A red coat lay nearby. Police found a large rock next to her body covered in blood and human tissue.

An autopsy determined that Lila had died after receiving multiple blows to the head delivered with enough force to severely fracture her skull.

As with the murders of the Pauls and Evelyn Roche, there was no robbery and even though the killer had ripped the clothes off Dorothy, Evelyn, and Lila, there was no evidence of sexual assault. Both Dorothy and Lila's heads had been wrapped in items of their own clothing.

DID VANCOUVER HAVE A SERIAL KILLER?

After the brutal murder of Evelyn Roche, police chief George Archer issued a warning that they were hunting a "sex fiend" who could strike again at any time. He warned women to travel in pairs, and if they had to travel alone, to arrange to be met by a male escort. It was the reason that David picked Helen up from the bus stop every night. As Neil Boyd, a criminology professor at Simon Fraser University says, Vancouver was still very much a small city in the '50s, and the possibility of three murderers at large seems highly improbable. "Predatory, sexual serial attacks are very rare and when there's a similarity and character over a relatively short period of time, that tends to point to the likelihood that we are looking for the same person."

Holly was a few years younger than Dorothy Pauls, but she remembers the adults of her neighbourhood talking about the murder. Some had children who went to school with Dorothy. "I was really young, but I do remember how much all the adults talked about it, I guess that's why I remember it," she says. "People just weren't prepared for such violence in their own neighbourhood. It was very sad."

Holly's family lived at Fraser near 57th, fairly close to the Pauls.

"Most people didn't even lock their doors," she says. "That all changed in our house after the murders. My dad put slide bolts on all the doors and windows. My brother, who was a teenager at the time, used to walk home from his girlfriend's house on Knight Street, cutting across 53rd to Fraser. I can remember my mother telling him over and over to *never* walk along 53rd again."

The Investigation

The only clues police had to go on in the Pauls' murder investigation were a partial footprint in the garden, a bloody but unidentifiable palm print on the wall, and a dislodged rock in the garden that indicated the way the killer had fled. The murder weapon was never found, but forensics determined that the bullets came from a Rohm RG-10 Revolver. Another dead end, as the guns were sold throughout the US for $14.95 under the brand name Rosco.

A neighbour told a *Province* reporter that he saw a 1950 blue Ford parked in the back lane near the Pauls' chicken coop on the night of the murder. A 13-year-old boy said he saw a blue car circling the block from his living room window. The driver, he said, was alone and had a mustache.

At one point police believed they had found their murderer when Bellingham Police arrested Henry Thompson, an 18-year-old First Nations boy from Mission, BC. Thompson was charged with the attempted rape of Bellingham resident Sharon Sharp, 11, and the sexual assault and murder of Ethel Tussing, also of Bellingham, who was walking home after dropping off her daughter at a babysitting job. The attacks happened four days after the Pauls murder, and newspapers of the time reported that Thompson had come to Bellingham via Vancouver. Although the murders were similar, Thompson was on Vancouver Island when the Pauls were murdered and police were unable to tie him to any of the Vancouver killings.

No Motive

Police followed up on a number of leads in the Pauls murder, but couldn't find a motive. A botched robbery and a potential home invasion were also ruled out, because while police initially thought David's wallet was missing, they later found he didn't carry one. Nothing else in the house was ransacked or even touched, including Helen's purse which lay open on the table. Police later found several hundred dollars hidden in jars and socks.

Another theory was that Dorothy was the target all along. A peeping Tom had been reported in the area around the same time, and there was the partial footprint outside her window. Police theorized that the peeper was caught by David as he watched Dorothy undress. Police also talked to a boy that Dorothy had a crush on, but he had an alibi, and barely knew she existed.

The Pauls were devout Mennonites, but had broken away from the church after David refused to tithe a percentage of his earnings over to the church. Mennonite officials were suspicious of police and unhelpful, but police ruled out that they had a motive for murder.

Neighbours speculated that it may have been a case of mistaken identity. The Pauls had bought the house from long-time residents Charles Geach, a police sergeant with the Vancouver Police Department, and his wife Violet. At 53, Geach was close in age to David Pauls and they also had a daughter, Barbara.

Joe Swan, a VPD police sergeant wrote about the murder in his book *Police Beat: 24 Vancouver Murders*. Swan said police investigated and dismissed a number of tips. One theory was that Helen Pauls' employer at the Home Fancy Sausage Shop was a "communist" and she had overheard a plot of some sort and threatened to inform on him. Another theory was that it was some unknown problem the Pauls had left behind in their native Russia. At one point, police took palm prints and applied a polygraph to a Russian man who the Pauls had stayed with when they first came to Vancouver.

None of these theories panned out. A $14,000 award offered by Woodwards, the *Vancouver Sun*, the Vancouver Police Commission, CKNW and Mayor Fred Hume was never claimed.

On April 21, 1965 Vancouver Police Officer Len Hogue, 34, drove to his Coquitlam home, took out a borrowed .357 magnum revolver and shot his wife Irene and his children Larry, 14, Noreen, 11, Ray, 8, Cliff, 7, Darlene, 4 and Richard, 3. He then placed the gun to his left temple and blew out his brains. Or did he?

WHEN COPS WERE ROBBERS

Constable Leonard Raymond Hogue was one of a gang of four rogue cops who supplemented their police paycheques through an escalating series of robberies. The first, which earned them the name the "ice cream bandits," began after only a few years on the job, when they started knocking over Dairy Queens. The pickings were easy but slim, and soon the four officers—Hogue, David Harrison, John Mc-Cluskey, and his brother-in-law, Joe Percival—had moved onto bigger scores and pulled off some of the biggest bank robberies in Vancouver's history.

Percival joined the police department in 1955, the year of the Mulligan Affair and when newspaper headlines and tales of corrupt cops rocked Vancouver. Perhaps a job on the force still looked like a good bet for like-minded individuals. Harrison, who was no choirboy, later described Percival as the "brains" behind the operations, and the smartest and most cold-blooded guy he'd ever met.

Hogue, Harrison and McCluskey all joined the Vancouver Police Department in 1956. Harrison never finished school and attached a forged high school diploma to his application. At 13, he found his father's body hanging from a beam in their Vernon garage. Three years later he crashed a car into a bridge in Montana. His mother was in the back seat and died a few days later. In 1956 he bought a two-year-old black low-rider Studebaker with the last of his inheritance and headed for Vancouver.

Hogue arrived from Winnipeg in 1954 with wife Irene and their two children, Larry and Noreen. They found a small place at 5711 Joyce, and Hogue got work as a salesman at Canadian Bakeries before joining the police department.

Both Percival and McCluskey were prison guards at Oakalla before joining the Vancouver Police Department in 1955 and 1956 respectively. McCluskey, Hogue, and Harrison all went through the police academy together.

Russell Reid also joined the VPD in September 1956 and was in the same class as McCluskey, Hogue and Harrison. He remembers that Hogue drove an old woodie station wagon, and although they worked in different areas—Hogue was taken off patrol and worked as a jailor—he liked him very much. When Reid brought in a prisoner they'd often talk about Hogue's growing family. "He'd say I can't even hang my pants over the bed and my wife gets pregnant," said Reid. Hogue, he said, was "straitlaced" and he still has trouble believing Hogue was involved in the robberies or the murders.

The robberies started simply enough. Hogue and Percival were on patrol and noticed that a Dairy Queen was left unlocked. After investigating they found a small bag of cash in the freezer. They took it with them. When they found out that it was policy for Dairy Queen franchisees to leave the day's take in the fridge, they got McCluskey and Harrison involved. Hogue even designed a piece of metal that would jimmy the locks.

From Burgers to Banks

As their confidence grew, so did the take. The cops robbed a Hunter's Sporting Goods on Kingsway. Their haul included 14 guns and ski masks which they would soon put to use in bank robberies.

The first job at the CIBC at Kingsway and McMurray branch in Burnaby on Christmas Eve, 1962, went off without a hitch. Hogue and Percival broke in through the back door of the bank shortly before 5:00 p.m. and Harrison drove the stolen getaway car. Armed with the stolen guns and a police radio, the men—described

as one tall and one short—entered the bank wearing trench coats and the stolen ski masks and scooped up $106,000 after a couple of minutes of terrorizing the bank staff.

Hogue had enough money to move his wife and six kids out of what friends had called a "small shack" into a large house on Harbour Drive in an upmarket area of Coquitlam.

By 1962, Harrison, who had bounced around to different addresses on the West Side, was living at impressive digs at 1990 West 19th Avenue. He quit his job, moved to Nelson and joined the local police. It was short-lived. A bad reference from the Vancouver Police Department got him fired, and for a time he worked as a private detective and as a car salesman.

McCluskey and his wife Audrey stayed put at 1138 Rose Street in Grandview-Woodlands. Percival and his wife Rose lived at 5550 Rugby Street in Burnaby. Percival left the force in November 1963 to sell real estate for Block Bros. He met James McDougall there, and introduced him to a business venture with higher stakes than real estate.

In June 1964, the gang knocked over the Simpson Sears on Kingsway, and the following January they robbed the Bank of Nova Scotia at Dunbar and West 41st Avenue.

The case of the mutilated bank notes
Things started to get really interesting when the gang learned of a $1.2 million shipment of cash that was scheduled to arrive at the CPR Merchandise Service on West Pender. The cash was old money taken out of circulation by the banks and on its way to the mint in Ottawa to be destroyed. The robbery was perfectly planned and executed.

above: David Harrison's house.
EVE LAZARUS PHOTO

right: $1.2 million of recovered cash stolen from the CPR Merchandise Service office, 1965.
PHOTO COURTESY VANCOUVER POLICE MUSEUM P03286

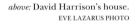

Harrison stole a getaway car—a white station wagon—and put an official sticker on the windshield. Hogue "borrowed" a police radio. To divert police attention away from their robbery, Harrison, claiming to be an RCMP officer, called the police department to report that a man was waving a gun around at the Hudson's Bay store.

Harrison, the driver, wore a light brown raincoat, a fedora and heavy horn-rimmed glasses. He stayed in the car. The other three—one dressed in the striped coveralls and cap of a railroad worker, one wearing a CPR police uniform, and the third wearing a blue police-type peaked cap and long blue coat—headed for the office.

One of the men pulled a long-barrelled gun, trained it on a clerk and told him: "If you don't do anything you won't get hurt." They bound him with rope and gagged his mouth with tape. The robbery was all over in 15 minutes, and they had pulled off what was then the largest heist in Vancouver's history.

What they didn't know was that the $1.2 million worth of cancelled bills had been drilled with three large holes and were virtually worthless.

Percival decided to risk it anyway. He cut sections from some bills and patched them onto others with clear adhesive tape, and starting passing them around. He didn't get away with it for long. On April 17, 1965, he was having a drink with McDougall at the Riviera Hotel in Edmonton when an alert bartender took a closer look at the tampered twenties. He called police.

ARREST OF PERCIVAL AND McDOUGALL FOR THEIR PART IN C.P.R. ROBBERY 1965.

Caught

When Edmonton police arrested Percival and McDougall, they found $12,000 made up of the patched twenties, the drilled bills and cash in the Travelodge room where they were staying. They also found a loaded .32 calibre semi-automatic pistol in a paper bag beside the bed that they later traced to the sporting goods store holdup.

Arrest photo of Joe Percival and James McDougall.
COURTESY VANCOUVER POLICE MUSEUM P00933

Hogue was at work when he found out about Percival and McDougall's arrest. He called McCluskey to warn him. Because Percival was a former Vancouver police officer, investigators began to look at his friends, and the phone call made them look hard at Hogue, who was already under suspicion.

Hogue had rented a station wagon to transport the money to a storage garage in Victoria and he knew that it was only a matter of time before police could prove his involvement. A few days after Percival's arrest, Hogue was driving on the freeway when his Volkswagon hit a curb and skidded 150 feet on its side at the Great Northern overpass. The car was a write off, but Hogue came away with just a cut on his forehead, which he had patched up at the Royal Columbian Hospital in New Westminster before going home. He called in and booked off that day of work. Police later believed that the car accident was a failed suicide attempt.

At first, Hogue's superiors weren't worried when the constable failed to turn up for work the next day, but after repeatedly telephoning his home, they became increasingly concerned.

Arrest photos of Joe Percival (left)
and James McDougall (right).
COURTESY VANCOUVER POLICE MUSEUM
P03297 AND P03298

Murder/Suicide

When Inspector Ted Oliver and Staff Sergeant H.C. Mutch arrived at Hogue's Coquitlam house they saw that the drapes were drawn and there were two newspapers piled on the doorstep. Nobody answered their repeated knocking. Inspector Oliver walked around the house, got down on his hands and knees and peered through the ground level basement window. There was a light on and he could just make out the body of a young girl lying on the Chesterfield, a bullet hole in her head.

All the doors and windows were locked and there were no signs of forced entry.

When police entered the house they found a basket of Easter eggs the kids had collected that Sunday morning. All three floors of the house were splattered with blood and eight bodies were spread throughout the house.

"The place was in a shambles, we kept finding bodies everywhere," a policeman told a reporter at the time.

Irene Hogue, 33, was the first to die at 1:30 am, shot through the back of her head while she slept. Larry, 14, was shot twice through the head while trying to get out of his top bunk bed. Raymond, 8, was murdered in the bathroom—the first shot missed and hit the toilet bowl. Clifford, 7, was killed while hiding in the small utility room.

At this point, the coroner determined, Hogue reloaded the .357 revolver and went down into the basement to find his daughters Noreen, 11, and Darlene, who was turning 5 in two days time. The girls died with a single shot to the back of their heads. Richard, 3, the baby of the family, was the last to die—murdered in his cot upstairs. Hogue went back to the master bedroom, and shot himself through the left temple with the gun and ammunition he had borrowed from a friend, a policeman who worked for the CPR. Problem was, Hogue was right-handed.

Former police officer Russell Reid is not the only cop who had a hard time believing that Hogue had murdered his family and killed himself. Many felt that Hogue was a victim of the real killer. A spokesperson for the city prosecutor's office told a *Province* reporter at the time of the murders that even if Hogue was implicated in the robbery and convicted, he would likely only have had to serve five years, and even then probably would have been out in three. However, a Coroner's Court ruled the deaths murder/suicide.

Simma Holt worked the police beat for the *Vancouver Sun* and knew all the officers involved. She followed the case quite closely, even visiting their graves several times over the years. "Nobody really followed up on that case, it was just left hanging," she said.

The only members of the Hogue family to survive the carnage were Cindy, a black lab retriever, and the children's pet hamster.

The Trial

The CPR policeman who admitted loaning Hogue his gun had worked with Percival as a guard at Oakalla prison. He told police that he may have mentioned the shipment to Percival or Hogue, but couldn't remember and was never linked to the robbery or charged. McCluskey was suspended from the police force and became a real estate agent with Dexter Realty. He was never charged, and died from a heart attack in 1987 at the age of 61.

At the preliminary hearing in July 1966, Percival, 37, Harrison, 32, and McDougall, 32, faced charges of armed robbery, possession of stolen money and conspiracy to steal money. McDougall and Percival were released on $6,000 bail and promptly fled to England, where they convinced the insurance company to pay them $60,000 in exchange for telling them where they stashed the rest of the mutilated money. They were extradited back to Vancouver and were sentenced to four years in jail for possession of stolen money.

Harrison was convicted of the train robbery, the bank heist and being in possession of $6,500 in stolen money. He received a 15-year sentence, but was released in 1970 and worked as a bouncer in a Gastown club. Harrison died in 1995 without ever being caught committing another crime.

On June 24, 1992 Jean Ann James, 53, a former flight attendant, went to the Shaughnessy home of her husband's wealthy lover and slit her rival's throat with a box cutter.

THE BILLIONAIRE'S DAUGHTER

The Jameses and the Wakabayashis were close friends. They often went to one another's houses with their children for dinner parties. Young Adam James and Elisa Wakabayashi were at the Montessori school together until Grade 3.

Derek James was a traffic controller at Vancouver International Airport and Shinji Wakabayashi was an executive with Japan Airlines. Jean Ann James was a former flight attendant with Canadian Pacific Airlines and on the union's executive. Gladys Wakabayashi, born Miao Feng Ling, was the third child of Taiwanese billionaire Y.S. Miao, chairman of Union Petrochemical Corp and the Lien Hwa Industrial Corp. She came to Canada in 1976 and married Shinji Wakabayashi two years later.

While the Wakabayashis house was a large eight-bedroom on Selkirk in Shaughnessy, it was still fairly average by the neighbourhood's standards. With Gladys's money, they could have afforded better, but they had family in the neighbourhood. Gladys's brother Hermi Miao and his wife Susanna Yang lived next door.

Gladys and Shinji split around 1990, but the Jameses and the Wakabayashis kept in close contact. Too close, as it happened. Jean believed she had found evidence that her husband was having an affair with the 41-year-old Gladys.

She didn't tell her husband or her friend that she knew.

Gladys Wakayashi's
Shaughnessy house.
EVE LAZARUS PHOTO

Slashed to Death

Jean phoned Gladys and told her that she had a present for her and wanted to bring it over to her home. Gladys had a piano lesson later that morning, so she invited Jean for coffee at 9:15 a.m., when she would return from dropping Elisa off at school.

Jean parked her car five blocks away and walked down the lanes at the back of the streets so she wouldn't be seen. Gladys let her in, they hugged, and Gladys made coffee. Jean told her that she wanted to give her a necklace, and the two friends went into Gladys's dressing room. Gladys sat on the stool while Jean slipped on a pair of gloves and pretended to take out the necklace. Instead of slipping the necklace around her neck, Jean slashed the other woman's throat with a box cutter. As Gladys slowly bled to death, Jean slashed her legs and said that if she told her the truth about the affair, she would call an ambulance and save her life. "Which of course I had no intention of doing," she said later.

Her high-heeled shoes left bloody footprints on the carpet and the tiled floor of the bathrooms, but Jean was more concerned about fingerprints on the dishes in the kitchen. She washed the coffee cups and wiped down all the surfaces she'd touched. She wasn't overly worried, because she and Derek were frequent visitors to the house and she knew police would likely find their fingerprints.

She took the box cutter and threw it away in a dumpster on the other side of town.

Elisa waited for two hours for her mother to pick her up after school that day. Her mother always arrived promptly at 3:00 p.m., and by 5:00 p.m. the 12-year-old was really starting to worry. She called her father to come pick her up. When they let themselves into the house they found Elisa's mother lying on her back in a pool of blood.

"It's the most gruesome murder I've ever seen," veteran Vancouver Police Detective Murn MacLennan told a reporter a few days later. "Everyone we talked to said she was well-liked, kind, and a compassionate lady. It had to be someone who hated her with a passion that's hard to imagine."

Police suspected Jean, but there was no forensic evidence linking her to the murder. Jean lawyered up and stayed out of jail for the next 20 years.

The Sting

In 2007, the Provincial Unsolved Homicide Unit began to woo Jean, now 69, in an ambitious undercover operation. The "Mr. Big" operation invented an entire crime ring, with police officers acting as gang members. Agents befriended Jean, met up with her at a spa, joined her gourmet club, took her to expensive restaurants to show how rich and powerful they were and eventually discussed her potential inclusion.

The sting went on for several months and took place across the country, ending in a Montreal hotel room in 2008.

Meetings were taped, and the tapes showed Jean embracing her new life of crime and the chance to earn a payoff in the hundreds of thousands of dollars. The icing on top was a movie role for her son, Adam, an aspiring actor. She was hooked—she even offered to kill for the gang, and to prove she had the chops, she told the man she thought was a crime boss the details of how she had slashed Gladys's throat.

Even allowing for the fact, as her lawyer later argued, that Jean was exaggerating her badassedness to impress the officer who she thought was a crime boss, the video of the meeting is chilling.

When the officer said he was surprised that a box cutter would do the job, she calmly told him the blade was similar to a surgeon's scalpel; it just couldn't go through bone.

At another taped meeting played at the trial, Jean is told about a fake kidnapping and beating of a man who owed the gang money. When the fake crime boss asked Jean what they should do, she told him to curl his penis with a curling iron, and then "cut his knackers off."

Jean told the undercover police officer that she had never told anyone what she had done, including her husband. "I never tell my husband my business," she said. "My mother always told me that if you have secrets, then keep them to yourself."

In fact, she said her husband, who was naturally upset at Gladys's death, never suspected her, even when the police focused their investigation on her. "I don't think he thinks I am capable of doing that," she said.

The Arrest

The James family lived in an unassuming two-storey house on a half-acre property on Bridge Street, Richmond, which they had bought in the 1980s. When police arrested Jean Ann James, a shocked next-door neighbour told the local newspaper that the senior citizen was an "absolute sweetheart of a lady," one of the best neighbours she'd ever had. Another neighbour told the reporter that the Jameses were generous and always had feeders out for the birds, and that Jean loved to garden.

After two decades, the former flight attendant was convicted of first-degree murder and sentenced to a minimum of 25 years. She lost her appeal in January 2013.

Elisa Wakabayashi moved to Taiwan with her aunt and uncle following the murder. She returned to Vancouver, married, and is now a yoga and spin instructor at a private Vancouver club. The house on Selkirk was listed for sale in 2005 for $1.2 million. Shortly after it sold, the number was changed—likely to avoid association with the brutal murder.

CHAPTER 10

Haunted Houses

House ghosts come in all sorts of shapes, sizes and sounds. Some people hear footsteps when no one else is home, others feel a presence, and some see an outline of the ghost. Sometimes the ghost is mischievous and hides things from the householders. Ghosts slam doors, fiddle with electrical appliances, wear perfume, smoke cigars and try to communicate with the living. A house may be haunted by a ghost that has unfinished business, or as a result of a traumatic event such as a murder or a suicide. Sometimes the ghost is benign and even helpful, and at other times it's downright malevolent.

One thing's for sure: to understand a ghost, it helps to know a little bit about the history of the house.

THE KITSILANO GHOST

Over the years, Nikki and Chris Renshaw have uncovered bits and pieces of their house's past. The King George V playing cards behind the kitchen wall, the sepia photos under the bathroom floorboards, names carved into the basement chimney and dozens of empty bottles of booze buried in the garden.

The 1912 craftsman on West 5th Avenue wasn't always a happy house, and at least one of the former inhabitants has stayed.

"There's been adultery, divorce, destitution, mental breakdowns and the odd death," says Nikki, a former radio personality who now designs luxury bedding.

Originally from London, England, the Renshaws bought their house in 1998

opposite: Children at Queen Mary Elementary school in North Vancouver wearing gas masks in 1941.
PHOTO #728 COURTESY NORTH VANCOUVER MUSEUM AND ARCHIVES

left: Current and past residents felt the ghost's presence on this landing.
EVE LAZARUS PHOTO

and put it through a massive renovation. They kept the stained glass windows and the wainscotting, but likely all the activity upset the ghosts, who made their presence known by brushing past them on the stairs. Chris, a set designer, would yell "It's only me," on entering the house. Glasses, keys and other small items disappeared. Lights turned on and off.

The bed shook so hard that Nikki would check for seismic activity. "This went on for about a month, until one night I sat bolt upright and shouted out, 'stop this immediately and go back to sleep,' in my best Mary Poppins voice. It never happened again."

In one of those freaky coincidences that happen when you start to investigate old houses, Nikki found that Denise, a Canadian she knew in London, grew up in the house next door. Denise's friend Laura Finlayson had lived in the Renshaw's house during the 1960s and '70s. When Laura came to visit, she asked Nikki if the ghost was still on the landing. Laura told her that she'd been so scared as a kid that she'd refused to use the upstairs bathroom.

Nikki has a few ideas of who the ghosts may be. There's Catherine Dickson, the first homeowner, who drank herself to death. Laura's Aunt Jean was hit by a tram on Fourth at Alma and died in the upstairs bedroom. Laura's father was often away at sea, and after she found a love letter from another woman in his suitcase, the family sold up and moved to Point Grey.

Nikki Renshaw at her haunted Kitsilano house. EVE LAZARUS PHOTO

THE GHOSTS OF BELLA VISTA

It's not surprising that ghosts stay around at Bella Vista; the place is a storybook cottage built on 100 acres of rolling green fields.

Bella Vista was built in 1920 by a Dr. Wessell, who used the farm as his weekend retreat. The farmhouse sits behind a large fence and cedar hedge on a busy stretch of highway and its steeply pitched shingled roof is clearly visible from the street.

Harry Reifel bought the property in 1930 with proceeds from his brewery and rum-running activities. There he bred jersey cows, ran a dairy and built a three-quarter-mile training track for racehorses.

Businessman and philanthropist Joe Segal bought the farm after Reifel died in 1973 and sold it to a group of investors a few years later. The investors subsequently flipped the property to the Cloverdale Raceway, which then rented it out to a series of tenants.

Debbie Pendergast was one of those tenants. She moved into the 4,600 square foot house in the early 1990s.

"My daughter wasn't quite a year yet when we moved in and I remember having to go down and get her bottle warmed up at night," says Debbie. "It was a big home, and I remember trying to go back up the stairs and you would feel like somebody was on your heels."

Debbie says the ghost wore perfume.

In the six years that she lived there, Debbie, who has four kids, tried never to go down into the basement. If she came home late she would park her car in the garage, slam the door and run into the house.

"You just felt that somebody was watching you constantly," she said. "It was a very eerie feeling."

The barns at Bella Vista.

Sometimes objects would be moved and other times she'd hear strange noises.

"I remember waking up out of a dead sleep in the middle of the night once because I could hear what sounded like an old grandfather clock ticking 'tick-tock, tick-tock,'" she says. "It went on for about five minutes. We couldn't find anything … it was just bizarre."

When Debbie moved in she found old booze bottles in the crawl space under the living room. She found an old mortar downstairs and had to call the police to come and remove it.

Shortly after Debbie moved there, one of her friends told her that the place was once a whorehouse. "My friend used to go there with his grandpa when he was a kid, and sit outside and wait."

One New Year's Eve, Debbie's mother visited and stayed alone at the house while Debbie went out. Debbie's mother was washing the dishes and looked up just in time to catch a glimpse of a very tall man in the mirror. "She made us come home because she was quite sure that she'd seen somebody," says Debbie. "It was definitely a creepy house."

THE MOLE HILL GHOSTS

In the 1960s, the City of Vancouver started buying up a mixture of Queen Anne and Edwardian houses along Comox Street in the West End, intending to bulldoze them and double the size of Nelson Park.

If the idea of demolition wasn't enough to rattle a few ghosts, one of the living residents, Blair Petrie, set about spearheading a five-year campaign to save the houses

in Mole Hill, an area that stretches in a square around Comox, Thurlow, Bute and Pendrell Streets. He carefully researched the past owners of the houses and wrote a book about the area. As part of his research, he made a couple of ghostly discoveries.

The Thurlow Street house was one of four built in 1903 by a doctor who went into real estate speculation, the favourite sideline of almost anyone with a few bucks at the time. He most likely flipped it straight away, and then it changed hands over the years to a number of different, mostly working class, residents.

When Blair started his research, the house was a bed and breakfast where strange things happened. The two owners would find lights turned on after they had turned them off, and once found a room locked from the inside. Most convincing were the actual sightings.

"They had both witnessed this ghost, and had many of their customers over the years come down to breakfast totally freaked out," says Blair.

The ghost only showed herself in one bedroom and always wore a high-necked period nightdress. She would be seen combing her long blonde hair in front of what was probably once a dresser. Most of the sightings were by women who stayed in that particular room. Once the ghost spoke to a guest and asked her: "Are you being taken care of here?"

Blair couldn't find anything in the house's history to explain the ghost. Now that the house has changed owners, been stripped to its studs, and remodelled into rental suites, he says he doesn't know whether the ghost stayed or moved somewhere more accommodating.

THE HAUNTING OF QUEEN MARY ELEMENTARY SCHOOL

The Queen Mary Elementary School was built in 1914 on Keith Road in North Vancouver. It has sheltered a couple of ghosts for much of the time since. Over the years, teachers have reported seeing a young boy of about six and an older man who looks like a school custodian. Diane, a Queen Mary teacher, has never seen the custodian, but she's seen the boy several times. He turns up in class from time to time, and once he was at the back of a lineup of kids. He was wearing blue coveralls and a blue plaid shirt that looked like it came from another era—possibly the 1950s or early '60s.

He looked at her and then disappeared. "He's quite mischievous," she says. "He only comes out when I am being very teacherly."

THE OSBORNE ROAD GHOST

When Jennifer and Patrick, and their children Graham, 6, and Angus, 3, moved into their North Vancouver home in 1998, they didn't realize they'd be sharing it with strangers. But to Jennifer, an interior designer, it soon became obvious that they weren't alone.

"We really had some very unusual experiences when we first moved in," she says. "We even contacted the previous owners to ask if they'd had any strange experiences and they said 'no, no, no, there was nothing, it's fine we never had anything unusual happen.'"

But things did happen. And they weren't easy to explain.

The boys each had their own room on the main floor of the house. "It made me a little anxious because they had always slept above us in the previous house," says Jennifer. "I was hyper aware of listening for them. There was one morning, it was very

early, around 4:30 a.m., and I could hear running in the hallway downstairs. I jumped out of bed and came downstairs and both the boys were fast asleep. The next day at the same time, I found my youngest outside in the driveway. There's no way he could have unlocked the door. The next day he woke up, came upstairs and said 'I can't sleep downstairs anymore because the boy and the girl are keeping me awake all night.'"

And other strange things happened. Jennifer had taken photos of the house when it first went up for sale. She says when they went back some time later to look at the photos, they could see a little face gazing out from the window that was now Angus's room.

"All of those things were unusual, but they could have explanations other than there was a ghost in the house, but at the time there were a lot of things," she says. "Doors were opening and closing—never when I could see them, but I could always hear them."

Four years before Jennifer and Patrick had bought the house, *North Shore News* reporter Dorothy Foster interviewed the owner at the time. She told Foster that she was working in the garden when a former owner drove up and told her that she had shared the house with two "entities." She described one as a lovely young woman and the other ghostly figure as an angry old man. The current owner told Foster that she didn't think much about the story until one day a friend came to visit and refused to come inside because she had a strange feeling about the house. The next day, the owner insisted this same friend come in for a cup of tea; the owner came out of the kitchen only to see her friend had bolted out of the house, jumped into her car and driven off. Later she told the owner that she'd seen a vision of a pretty young woman dressed in black in the living room, and then was confronted by the apparition of an angry old man on the stairs.

opposite top: Residents have come and gone from these Mole Hill houses over the years. Sometimes they stay around.
EVE LAZARUS PHOTO

opposite bottom: Queen Elizabeth Elementary school, in North Vancouver.
EVE LAZARUS PHOTO

above: These North Vancouver ghosts only appear in times of renovation or upheaval.
EVE LAZARUS PHOTO

Jennifer wasn't able to find any explanation for the ghosts when she researched the past owners, but she's sure that it was two children. After a few months, everything stopped, and she figures that the move disturbed the presence somehow. "It was all kind of bizarre."

Former resident described her house as a "very unlucky place."
EVE LAZARUS PHOTO

THE GHOSTS OF GLEN DRIVE

Ernie McLeod, a millworker, and his wife Kellsie bought their house on Glen Drive in 1948 and moved in there with their small daughter Nowell. It wasn't long before they found out they weren't alone.

"We used to hear footsteps," Kellsie said. "I heard them, my husband heard them, my daughter heard them, a guest we had once heard them. It was from the front door to the kitchen door in the lower hall and it sounded like an old, tired man with heavy shoes on."

The McLeod's son Morrin was born in 1950.

By the time Nowell was five she was sleeping in the upstairs bedroom off the hall, close to the stairs. She'd wake up terrified during the night and tell her mother that a man was leaning over her bed. Kellsie thought her little girl was seeing the flashing lights from cars going by, until her own mother came to stay over and help look after the kids after Kellsie miscarried twins.

"My mother came downstairs and she looked awful," said Kellsie. "She said she couldn't sleep. She kept waking up because she said that there was an old man leaning over her."

Kellsie said she could never find an explanation or discover if any of the past residents had died there and decided to stay around. "It was a very unlucky place," she said.

Once Kellsie was in the pantry and suddenly had a feeling that somebody was watching her.

"I was absolutely terrified. Finally I turned around and of course there was nobody there. I reached over to pick up the lid of a casserole and it seemed as though the lid jumped at me, it broke my knuckle and blood hit the ceiling and I remember thinking after I got stitched up 'this is it, it's time that we left'." Fifty years later, she still had the scar.

The McLeods sold the house in 1953 and moved to another on Windsor, leaving the ghosts behind. Morrin was 23 when he died in a car accident at Ashcroft in 1973. His father died four weeks later from severe pulmonary emphysema. Kellsie died in 2008 at the age of 91.

Three decades after the McLeods left the neighbourhood, Jose Lee and her sister bought the blue house across the road. They lived there for a time with their mother, a family friend, and the uninvited previous tenant who had died some years before.

When Jose Lee bought her house in 1984, she said it had the most beautiful landscaping in the neighbourhood. "There were roses of various colours, multicoloured foliage, and the yard had an undulating lawn covered by well-manicured grass," she said.

The house has four bedrooms—one upstairs and three in the basement.

Shortly after they moved in, the women realized that there was something off about the house. It was 6:00 p.m. and they heard a clicking at the mail slot, as if someone was checking for mail. When Jose looked, no one was there. The same sound happened every night at precisely 6:00 p.m., usually while they were eating dinner. "I would look at my watch and I would tell everyone: 'two minutes to six'—and two minutes later the mail slot would click. It happened every day except during the weekend."

Once, when Jose was alone in the house, she was brushing her teeth before going to bed when she heard heavy footsteps. She thought it was a burglar.

"I kept quiet and turned off the bathroom light and kept the door ajar. If it was an armed thief I thought I could protect myself by slamming the door on him," she said. "I listened as the footsteps went down to the basement, and suddenly the footsteps stopped."

Jose looked out, and to her surprise, caught a glimpse of a man's back as he passed. He had blonde hair and was wearing a pair of jeans and a white shirt. She thought he looked to be in his late 60s. "What was really weird was that he made no sound, and he appeared to be floating, because from the knees down, there was no image of his legs and feet," she said. "As I got out of the bathroom to follow him, he vanished before my eyes."

A few weeks later, Jose says she woke up around 2:00 a.m. thinking of the word "Rosicrucians," and having no idea what it meant. Later that day, she was cutting the grass when an older lady stopped to introduce herself as a long-time resident of the area. She told Jose that a widowed Dutchman used to own the place and always had the best garden in the neighbourhood. After he died, his son sold the house.

One former resident with a penchant for gardening refused to move out of his house after he died.
EVE LAZARUS PHOTO

"I asked her if he was a member of a club or a group," says Jose. The woman told her that he was, and that she believed that it was a group like the Freemasons, but they called themselves Rosicrucians.

"I told my mother and my sister that the Dutchman was beginning to involve me in whatever agenda he was having and I had no plans to accept his invitation," she said.

They sold the house.

"For some reason I sometimes have the urge to see the house again, so from time to time, I drive by," she says. "I stop for a few seconds, look at the house, feel very sad, and then I leave."

CHAPTER 11

West Coast Modern

"Modernism is a beautiful failure. You can't call it a success when 96 percent of people do not want to live in a modernist house." —Coast Modern documentary, 2012.

By the 1940s, Vancouver was melding architecture with art and design and producing a new group of artist and architects who were breaking away from traditional enclosed forms of housing. Many of these architects studied at the Vancouver School of Art and were influenced by artists such as Frederick Varley and Lawren Harris, founding members of the Group of Seven, as well as B.C. Binning, an artist who taught architectural design and is credited with kick-starting the West Coast Modern movement in Vancouver.

FREDERICK HORSMAN VARLEY (1881-1969)

Rice Lake Road, North Vancouver

In 1932, Fred Varley was sketching in his favourite North Vancouver spot when he noticed a small house high up on the bank of Lynn Creek. He tried to get through the forest to explore it, but couldn't find a road that would take him there. The next time he came, he saw that the weeds had been cut back along the side of the road and he could see a small path leading to the cottage.

Varley walked around the place, peered in the windows and saw that it was deserted. The boxy little house was in rough condition. It had porches tacked on to the front and back and an unfinished room on the main floor. He climbed up on the verandah and looked out over the valley and saw Mt. Seymour and Lynn Peak. When he looked down he saw a deep narrow canyon below.

To his delight, the house came with a piano and was available for $8 a month. He could commute to Vancouver by streetcar and ferry.

"That was the happiest time," Varley told a reporter 20 years later. "The only place in the world that I truly felt was mine."

Frederick Horsman Varley was an incredibly talented artist, a more-than-decent teacher, and as a founder of the Group of Seven, he was a Canadian icon. He was

left: BC Electric Head Office, 1957.
SELWYN PULLAN PHOTO

above: Maud Varley at Rice Lake Road, ca. 1960s.
PHOTO COURTESY OF LIZ JOHNSTON

above: The Group of Seven with
Frederick Varley at far left.
PHOTO: ARTHUR S. GOSS

below: Rice Lake House, 2014.
EVE LAZARUS PHOTO

also an irresponsible alcoholic who loved women, and—with his handsome face, clear blue eyes and a shock of copper-red hair—women loved him back.

None of this was much consolation to his wife Maud and their four children, Dorothy, John, Jim and Peter. The family were evicted from two rented Kitsilano homes in the short time they'd lived in Vancouver, and were about to be abandoned for Varley's current mistress, 19-year-old Vera Weatherbie.

Varley had moved out to BC in 1926 to teach at the Vancouver School of Decorative and Applied Arts—the forerunner to Emily Carr University of Art + Design. Varley had never held down a teaching job for more than a year, and he was not as productive as other members of the Group of Seven. Varley would have been thrilled by a salary of $3,000 a year—twice what he was making at the Ontario College of Art—and to have the opportunity to paint and sell the rugged West Coast scenery.

His salary allowed him to buy more than just paint; he indulged in expensive gin, brandy and beer for himself (and probably for many of his friends, because as his children later recalled, their father's salary didn't go to rent, education or clothes.)

By 1933, Vancouver was deep into the Depression. Faced with reduced hours and a huge cut in salary, Varley opened the BC College of Arts with Jock MacDonald. The following year, he left Maud and the kids to fend for themselves, and rented the cottage on Rice Lake Road in Upper Lynn Valley.

The next three years were supposedly his spiritual high point. Varley painted *Dharana, Birth of Clouds, Lynn Creek, The Trail to Rice Lake* and *Weather-Lynn Valley*—many from the second storey window of his house.

When Varley left for Ottawa, Maud, Jim and Peter moved into the house. In 1937, she received a small inheritance from her mother and used the money to buy the house and add a bathroom and bedroom.

Dorothy and her daughter Liz moved in to take care of Maud, and kept the house until Dorothy's death in 1974.

Peter's son Chris Varley, an art dealer, visited many times. He spent a week there with his grandmother in the summer of 1962. "It was indeed a magical spot, although in seriously dilapidated condition," he says. "At that time it was still stuffed with Varley's paintings and drawings. *Church at Yale*, now in the BC Archives, hung in the stairwell."

Chris Varley says he remembers an unframed portrait of his Aunt Dorothy wrapped in a green garbage bag and stored under the kitchen sink.

"There was an old bureau with a drawer full of scattered, unmatted drawings," he says. "An early Tom Thomson sketch was reputedly used to patch a leak in the ceiling of the attic, which was also my grandfather's studio."

Three years after Varley returned to eastern Canada, Lawren Harris, another founding member of the Group of Seven, arrived in Vancouver.

LAWREN STEWART HARRIS (1885–1970)
4760 Belmont Avenue, Vancouver

Of all the Group of Seven artists, Lawren Harris was the only one born rich. He grew up in Brantford, Ontario, studied in Germany where he discovered theosophy, came home, married more money, had three children, and produced sought after works of art.

And then things fell apart. He fell in love with Bess, the wife of his friend, and the two fled to Santa Fe. Then in 1940 they settled in Vancouver to be close to his mother Annie, who lived in Victoria.

Harris had always been a staunch supporter of Canadian art and his arrival made a huge impact on provincial Vancouver. His own painting was evolving from impressionist-influenced landscapes to abstract works.

The Harrises bought the house on Belmont, and every second Saturday held a musical evening, inviting up to 30 people to sit in their living room and listen to records on one of the best sound systems in the city. Bess, often wearing a long white form-fitting dress, would sit on a white Angora goat-hair mat on the floor. Afterwards, she served drinks and sandwiches.

"You sat for three hours in the dark listening to an extraordinary collection of records on probably the finest hi-fi set up in the city, with very interesting people," Arthur Erickson told author Edith Iglauer in 1981. "I was 16 and terribly flattered to be included. A whole different world opened up to me."

Not much of the original house remains. According to Greatestates.info, current owner Anthony von Mandl of Mission Hill Family Estates bought the adjacent property, added an acre of garden, an underground garage with a green roof, and put the old house through a massive renovation that placed it as the fourth most expensive residence in Vancouver with a market value of $29 million.

In 2001 Canadian billionaire Ken Thomson paid $2.2 million for *Baffin Island*, and seven years later another Harris painting, *The Old Stump, Lake Superior*, fetched $3.5 million at auction.

In 1969, Harris was made a Companion of the Order of Canada. He still worked at his easel for three hours in the morning, gardened or walked after lunch and worked for another hour in the late afternoon.

B.C. Binning studied under Varley at the Vancouver School of Art and became friendly with the Harrises soon after they moved to Vancouver. As a teacher and mentor to future architects such as Ron Thom, Fred Hollingsworth and Arthur Erickson, he helped change how Canadians thought of design.

Lawren Harris.
COURTESY OF CITY OF VANCOUVER ARCHIVES CVA 371-3

137

BERTRAM CHARLES BINNING (1909–1976)
2968 Mathers Crescent, West Vancouver

Almost immediately after graduating from the Vancouver School of Art in 1929, B.C. Binning began to teach both art and his special interest, a course on architectural design.

Both Binning's grandfathers were architects, and throughout his career as an artist he always maintained that the discipline of architecture, with its dependence on a strong sense of organization and structure, informed his approach to drawing, painting and mural design.

"He taught me the beauty of the less detail, the better," Arthur Erickson said after taking a drawing course from Binning.

Ron Thom studied art at the Vancouver School of Art in the 1940s and has said that Binning was one of the most important influences in his life and the reason he switched from art to architecture. Binning, Thom once said, taught that every aspect of design had to respond to the world around it—whether that was colour, form, light or views, and it had a profound effect on everything he did.

In 1941, with the help of his friend and architect Ned Pratt, Binning designed the house where he and his wife Jessie would live for the rest of their lives. He sought out exposed cedar, Douglas fir, concrete floors and other local materials, and stunned people with his house's simple form, flat roof and the way he merged architectural features with art using a series of large colourful murals painted onto the walls of his house.

The house cost him $5,000.

Binning's murals adorn a number of important downtown buildings. One of his most famous was for Pratt's BC Electric Building in 1955. Binning designed a mural of dramatic elongated diamond shapes coloured blue, green and grey for the outside wall. Three years later, he designed a mural to celebrate BC's booming resource-based economy for the Imperial Bank of Commerce (CIBC). The 44-foot long mural, made from 200,000 pieces of Venetian glass, now belongs to the Shoppers Drug Mart at Granville and Dunsmuir Streets in downtown Vancouver.

Jessie lived in the house until her death in 2007 at 101. The couple didn't have children, and the house was left in the care of The Land Conservancy, where it is occasionally opened to the public. At the time of writing, the Binning house was the subject of a court challenge between UBC and The Land Conservancy and its future looked uncertain.

B.C. Binning designed this mural to celebrate BC's booming economy for the CIBC in 1958.
PHOTO ©2014 DEREK VON ESSEN

CHARLES EDWARD PRATT (1911–1996)
430 Stevens Drive, West Vancouver

Ned Pratt may be the most important architect to come out of Vancouver. As the principal of Thompson Berwick Pratt, he hired and mentored some of the most influential architects of the time. Arthur Erickson, Ron Thom, Paul Merrick, Barry Downs and Fred Hollingsworth all cut their teeth at TBP.

"He really championed modern architecture," says his son Peter Pratt. "He was never afraid to hire someone who was smarter than him and he was able to influence people."

Ned Pratt's crowning achievement was winning the commission to design the BC Electric building on Burrard Street—a game changer in the early 1950s. He was an architect who must have inspired trust because it was a radical departure for designers of the time that were still hanging onto traditional themes from the past.

"Pratt convinced BC Electric that a local firm with no experience in skyscraper design could handle the monumental task," architectural critic Robin Ward wrote in Pratt's obituary. "BC Electric was persuaded to ditch an early square-edged tower idea for an adventurous and elegant diamond-shaped floor plan achieved by an ingenious central structural shaft."

The drawings alone, if spread out, would have covered five city blocks, noted Ward.

Pratt also designed UBC's Graduate Centre and he likely brought his skills as an athlete into his design of the Memorial Gym at UBC. Pratt had been a rower. In 1932, he and his partner brought home a Bronze Medal for Canada at the Summer Olympic Games in Los Angeles.

While Pratt's commercial buildings stand as a testament to his design skills, it was his ideas for post-war inexpensive residential housing that would make a lasting impact.

When a client couldn't pay his bill in the early 1950s, Pratt accepted an acre lot in West Vancouver's British Properties instead. He built his own post-and-beam house designed on a four foot-by-eight-foot high module with plywood panels and a flat roof. Pratt even used leftover blue and yellow glass from the construction of the BC Electric building for one of his windows.

above: Ned Pratt, ca. 1960s.
SELWYN PULLAN PHOTO

right/below: Peter Pratt restored his father's house (right) and built a post and beam next door.
EVE LAZARUS PHOTO

"It wasn't so much the house that was important, it was the idea behind the house," says Peter. "He found an industrialized solution to housing."

When Peter, who is also an architect, took over the house after the death of his father, it had started to leak and rot. "I don't know how many times I heard 'it's a tear down Pratt, you can't save it'," he said. "This is our home, it's not so much an asset, it's our home. It has a sense of place."

Against all advice, Peter decided to save what he could and restore it. He moved walls around, took out rooms, added skylights and put cork on the floor. He added bench seats made from reclaimed wood from the old Pantages Theatre on East Hastings Street to go with a table his father built, and he saved an experimental mural that his father and Ron Thom made from paper, coloured dyes and fibreglass.

Peter has built his own post-and-beam home right next door. One side of the house is sheer glass and opens up onto the garden and a large water feature filled with fish. A courtyard connects the two houses and there are angles everywhere you look that give different scenic points of view. Ned's house is now around 1,200 square feet. Peter's is only slightly larger. Both are a nod to simplicity and scale and the importance of landscape.

RON THOM (1923–1986)

3600 Glenview Crescent, North Vancouver

When Kerry McPhedran put the Ron Thom house she'd owned for 40 years on the market, it wasn't by choice. For Kerry, a freelance writer, her West Vancouver home was also her retirement plan. But she didn't want to sell to a developer who would rip it down for the land value; the house had nurtured her when she needed it and she wanted an owner who would love it as much as she did.

"If you have lived in one of these houses, you do feel your life is better having lived in that space," she said.

Ron Thom built Kerry's house on Duchess Street in 1954 for Joan and Bruce Boyd, friends and artists who studied with him at the Vancouver School of Art. Kerry was the third owner. Her office was in the same room where the Boyds once painted, and where the second owner, a voice coach, kept her piano.

Long before Thom designed the Massey College, the Shaw Festival Theatre and the Toronto Zoo, he designed more than 60 houses, mostly on the North Shore. Many of these were bulldozed, including the Lynn Valley house that he built for his own family in 1948.

Thom originally wanted to be a concert pianist. He practiced for several hours a day. He entered competitions, often winning or placing, but after his mid-teens he never played in public again. He never lost his love for the piano, and he designed a number of the houses with rooms designed to hold a grand piano, even for clients like the Boyds who didn't own or play a piano themselves.

In 1952 Thom designed a small experimental house for his family built from prefabricated plywood panels. He used ox-blood coloured concrete for the floors and installed floor-to-ceiling windows to flood the house with light. The house blends into the landscape and has views of the valley and Mosquito Creek.

top: Ron Thom, ca. 1950s.
SELWYN PULLAN PHOTO

above: Ron Thom designed this small North Vancouver house for his family in 1952. EVE LAZARUS PHOTO

Part tree house,
part Winnie the Pooh.
PHOTO COURTESY
JEANETTE LANGMANN

The home that Paul Merrick built for his family of six in the early 1970s has Ron Thom's old drafting table for its front door.

PAUL MERRICK
5762 Larson Place, West Vancouver

Jeanette Langmann, a Vancouver art dealer and Merrick House custodian, describes her soaring post-and-beam house as part tree house, part Winnie the Pooh. The kitchen, she says, gives the feeling of being inside a wooden boat.

"Living in this house is a lifestyle, it is your life and it becomes who you are," she says. "There is a calmness to the house and a serenity and there's an honesty to it. I feel happy and calm and at peace."

Jeanette, her husband Alastair Johnston, a builder, their two sons Benjamin and Nicholas, a yellow Lab and Bengal cat moved into the house in 2012.

"We just fell in love with the feeling of the house, and I wanted that for my family," she says.

Born in West Vancouver, Paul Merrick designed this home for his family in 1974. His goal was to create an interesting house on a modest budget, and do it without taking out one of the 36 Douglas Fir, Cedar, Hemlock and Maple trees on the sloping West Vancouver lot.

"It was not an uncommon issue. Ron Thom, Fred Hollingsworth, Ned Pratt, Barry Downs—we were trying to build houses that were interesting, but essentially simple," says Merrick. "I was trying to put a building in without challenging a tree and I wanted to create a very small structural footprint on what was a rock outcropping."

It's a magical kind of place and a fine example of the West Coast Style of contemporary architecture. The original structure was less than 900 square feet. Later, Merrick designed an addition incorporating cedar, stone and glass, and recycled building materials. There are soaring ceilings, multiple levels and exterior decks that blur the indoors with the outdoors. There is floor to ceiling Arts and Crafts stained glass in the living area, stunning views of Eagle Harbour and exposed natural rock in the basement. It's a place designed to look up. Built on a rocky promontory and nestled within a quarter-acre of private forest, much of the house has the feel of standing in a tree canopy.

Merrick interned at Thompson Berwick Pratt and became a full partner in 1968. He worked with Ron Thom, and when the BC Electric building was renovated into the Electra in 1993, it was Merrick who was the architect in charge of the restoration.

Merrick says the BC Electric building was part of a golden age of architecture in the Pacific Northwest.

"Nothing had ever been seen here like it before," says Merrick. "It was the compilation of the work of the best architects Vancouver had."

Merrick's heritage projects include the renovations to the Marine Building, the Orpheum Theatre and the former Bank of Montreal, now the Segal School of Business for Simon Fraser University. Merrick also designed Cathedral Place, the building which replaced the Georgia Medical Dental building demolished in 1989.

BARRY DOWNS
6664 Marine Drive, West Vancouver

In 1979 Barry Downs bought a piece of land on a rocky bluff, 120 feet above West Vancouver's Garrow Bay. Then he set about designing a house that would blend in with the landscape.

Downs's house is almost invisible from the busy street and built on multiple levels, with lots of glass that connects the indoors with the out.

Each step through the house is like a journey of discovery. A window in the bathroom looks out onto the forest. Another window gives a view of Bowen Island, another window gives a glimpse of the rocky exterior. But it's not until you step into the dining room that you can truly understand the brilliance of Downs' design. The Strait of Georgia, Vancouver Island and the BC coastline leap out through floor-to-ceiling glass windows, and just for a moment it's disorienting, like being suspended in space.

"To me, it's all to do with emotion, and you derive that from the building and its setting," says Downs. "The focus for me has always been the landscape, the garden, the seasonal world."

After graduating from the University of Washington in 1958, Downs moved back to Vancouver, was hired by Ned Pratt and put to work with some of the city's most exciting and imaginative architects.

"Everybody was there [Thompson Berwick Pratt] at one time or another," he said. "Erickson had already been fired, mostly everybody was fired after awhile."

"We built on narrow lots with simple and affordable post-and-beam houses," says Barry Downs. BARRY DOWNS PHOTO

Downs left TBP in 1963 and formed a four-year partnership with Fred Hollingsworth. And then in 1969 he and Richard Archambault launched their own company with residential houses as their mainstay.

"We built on narrow lots with simple and affordable post-and-beam houses. We designed houses that pushed up through the trees, that revolved around the idea of the big room, surrounded by the garden, and the view of the changing seasons," says Downs.

In the Downs' house, an outside deck accessed through the bedroom feels like an extension of the interior.

"It's all about embracing the rock, not mimicking it, but referencing it in terms of its modulation and its characteristics," he says. "Rock is always part of the interior as well as being a strong and powerful element and so that's how the house moves in and out and up and down because of those layers in topography."

A huge Gordon Smith painting hangs in the dining room and pulls the decor together. The artist is a good friend of the Downses and lives nearby, in a house designed by Arthur Erickson.

Downs, a soft-spoken man in his 80s, is as low-key as his buildings. He'd just like to see more of them remain.

"It's sad," he said. "I'd say 50 percent of modernist houses are torn down."

While Arthur Erickson, Ned Pratt, Barry Downs and Ron Thom have imprinted their West Coast style of architecture all over Vancouver, Fred Thornton Hollingsworth is the architect most responsible for the look of postwar North Vancouver.

FRED HOLLINGSWORTH
1205 Ridgewood Drive, North Vancouver

Lee Atwell grew up in a Hollingsworth house. Her parents bought the "Watts Residence" from the original owners in 1965 and her father lived in the house until his death in 2011. "I feel not only was it my parents who influenced our aesthetic tastes and deep connection to the natural world, but also the house itself. The house helped to define who we are today," she said.

Lee and her sister Bev's fear was that new owners would want to raze the place and put up something new. So they were immensely relieved when they found buyers who also loved the house. Instead of tearing it down, they hired Hollingworth's son Russell to design an addition in keeping with his father's philosophy.

Hollingsworth invented the Neoteric style where Lee, Bev and their older brother grew up—affordable family housing with a small footprint, open plan and simple post-and-beam construction. As early as 1946, Hollingsworth was including radiant floor heating, clerestory windows and skylights to let in lots of light.

Fred Hollingsworth in the Trethewey Residence he designed in 1961.
SELWYN PULLAN PHOTO

As Lee will tell you, a Hollingsworth house is part design, part art and part architecture.

Hollingsworth studied at the Vancouver School of Decorative and Applied Arts in 1929 and articled with Ned Pratt from 1946 to 1951. He started a collective of like-minded architects he dubbed "the intellects" which included Downs and Erickson.

"I've always said a home is an escape from the world; a place to which you escape to reconnect with nature," Hollingsworth told writer and urban designer Bob Ransford. "My clients were all individuals. I tried to get into their lives. I tried to find out how they used their space."

The houses were dubbed "midnight specials" because Hollingsworth and Thom designed them for $100 each, late at night while moonlighting from their day jobs at TBP.

Hollingsworth still lives in the North Vancouver house that he designed for his family in 1946. While he is known for his contemporary architecture and small residential homes, his architectural range is astounding. He designed UBC's Faculty of Law building in 1971 (now demolished), and in 1993, he designed Nat Bosa's waterfront mansion on South Oxley Street in West Vancouver.

Like many of the modern architects, Hollingsworth was inspired by Frank Lloyd Wright. He met the legend in 1951 and turned down a job offer to work with him, opting instead to develop his own style. He told a reporter for *Canadian Architect* that he wanted to stay in a small architectural practice.

Fred Hollingsworth designed Selwyn Pullan's studio in 1960.
SELWYN PULLAN PHOTO

"We're romantics and it is to me exciting to see a family raised in a fine building they have lived in since the day they were born," he said.

SELWYN PULLAN
233 Wooddale Road, North Vancouver

While Hollingsworth and the others were producing houses that were full of glass and angles, natural materials, and built to expand into spaces in ways unseen before, it was Selwyn Pullan who captured their vision.

After serving in the Canadian Navy during the Second World War, Pullan moved to Los Angeles to study photography at the Art Center School. One of his instructors was the legendary photographer Ansel Adams. After graduation, Pullan went to work as a news photographer at the *Halifax Chronicle*, and by the time he returned to Vancouver in 1950, he found a new movement of artists and architects who were reinventing the house. Pullan reinvented architectural photography.

When he found that the Speed Graphic was inadequate for the movement needed for photographing this new style of architecture, Pullan built his own camera. He quickly became a sought-after commercial photographer, working for magazines such as *Western Homes and Living, Macleans* and *Architectural Digest*.

"I just look at the house and photograph it," he shrugs. "I don't have any preconceptions when I photograph, it's a journalistic assignment not a photographic one."

His photos evoke a sense of time, optimism for the future, and perhaps even a new way of thinking. He intuitively understood the work of these architects, emphasizing light and space and often pulling in the homeowners and their children to show how the architectural and interior design fit with family life. His pictures show Gordon Smith painting in the studio designed by Arthur Erickson, a young Erickson lounging in his own adapted garage, and Jack Shadbolt painting in his now-demolished Burnaby studio.

In 1952, Pullan bought a house on a forested slope in North Vancouver. Pullan asked his long-time friend Fred Hollingsworth to design a carport. The finished structure, where he still parks his 1963 Jaguar, sits next to the house and looks more like a plane than a garage, and that's interesting not just from an architectural point of view, but because he and Hollingsworth used to make model airplanes together as teens. Pullan says Hollingsworth still does.

Selwyn Pullan in his studio, 2008.
KENNETH DYCK PHOTO

In 1960, when Pullan needed a multi-purpose studio and darkroom for his growing photography business, he sought out Hollingsworth again. Rather than add another room to the house, the architect created a covered passageway that led from the house and flowed down the slope of the property. He designed a two-level studio with floor-to-ceiling windows and concrete floors that blend seamlessly in with the landscape.

Six decades later, Pullan still lives in the house.

There's a grand piano in the studio left over from the '70s when Pullan was on the cutting edge of digital recording, and the room is filled with lights and props and dozens of photographs of people, and fashion and designer furniture, and art stacked in piles against the walls.

The book that Lawren Harris published in 1969—the year before he died—rests on the piano. Pullan shot the paintings that span the artist's career, from his early days with the Group of Seven through to his abstract period in Vancouver. Pullan refused to shoot them anywhere except in his studio and only when he was alone. The paintings would be trucked to his studio in batches, taken away and a new group brought in.

"I had millions of bucks worth of paintings in my studio back then." he said.

ARTHUR ERICKSON (1924–2009)
4195 West 14th Avenue, Vancouver
Of all the architects mentioned, Arthur Erickson is the one most widely known. His fingerprints are all over several of the city's most iconic buildings—Simon Fraser University on Burnaby Mountain, Robson Square, the Museum of Anthropology at UBC, and dozens of residential houses.

Erickson had taken a painting course from B.C. Binning at the Vancouver School of Art and initially wanted to become an artist. He was strongly influenced by Lawren Harris and one of his first jobs was designing a deck for the artist's Belmont Avenue home.

By 1957, with his career already well-established, he was teaching architecture at UBC and casting around for a place to live.

Unusually for an architect, Erickson chose not to design his own house, but bought a large corner lot with a small cottage and a garage in Point Grey for $11,000, out of which he created the 900-square-foot home where he lived for the next 52 years.

"Architecturally this house is terrible, but it serves as a refuge, a kind of decompression chamber," he told author Edith Iglauer.

He replaced the walls with sliding glass and connected the buildings, adding a bathroom and a kitchen. He played with different materials—leather tiles on the bathroom wall, wall tiles in Italian suede in the living room, and Thai silk in the study—and then he turned his attention to the garden.

Erickson bulldozed the English garden, dug a hole for the pond and used the dirt to make a hill high enough to block the view of his house from his neighbours.

"Everybody in the neighbourhood thought I was excavating to build a house, and chatted with me over the picket fence, very happy to believe that they were no longer going to have a nonconformist garage dweller among them," he told Iglauer.

He planted grasses and rushes from the Fraser River, pine trees from the forest, put in 10 different species of bamboo, and added rhododendrons, a dogwood, and a persimmon to the existing fruit trees. He was known for throwing lavish garden parties that drew a guest list ranging from Pierre Trudeau to Rudolf Nureyev.

Barry and Mary Downs lived in the Dunbar area at the time and knew Erickson quite well.

"We both had little ponds full of fish and one day Mary and I gave him a turtle," said Downs. "He phoned me up and said 'get over here your turtle is eating my fish!'"

"Arthur was ruthless. He had a BB gun and would shoot at the herons that would come in and land and eat his fish," says Barry Downs.
SELWYN PULLAN PHOTO, 1959

Down's told him that was impossible, the turtle had a mouth the size of Erickson's thumb.

"I went over and sure enough there's a fish sticking out of its mouth," said Downs, adding that, yes, he took the turtle back.

"Arthur was ruthless. He had a BB gun and would shoot at the herons that would come in and land and eat his fish. Once he told me that he shot through the neighbour's window accidentally," says Downs.

Downs says the impressive Japanese-inspired marble terrace panels in the garden are from the toilet stalls in the old Hotel Vancouver.

Erickson may have been a talented architect, but he was hopeless with finances. By 1992 he had racked up over $10 million in debt and was on the verge of losing his house. A group of friends, which included Peter Wall, took over the $475,000 mortgage and placed the house and garden in the hands of the Arthur Erickson Foundation. Erickson lived there until his death in 2009. Like most tiny houses on big lots, its future looks grim.

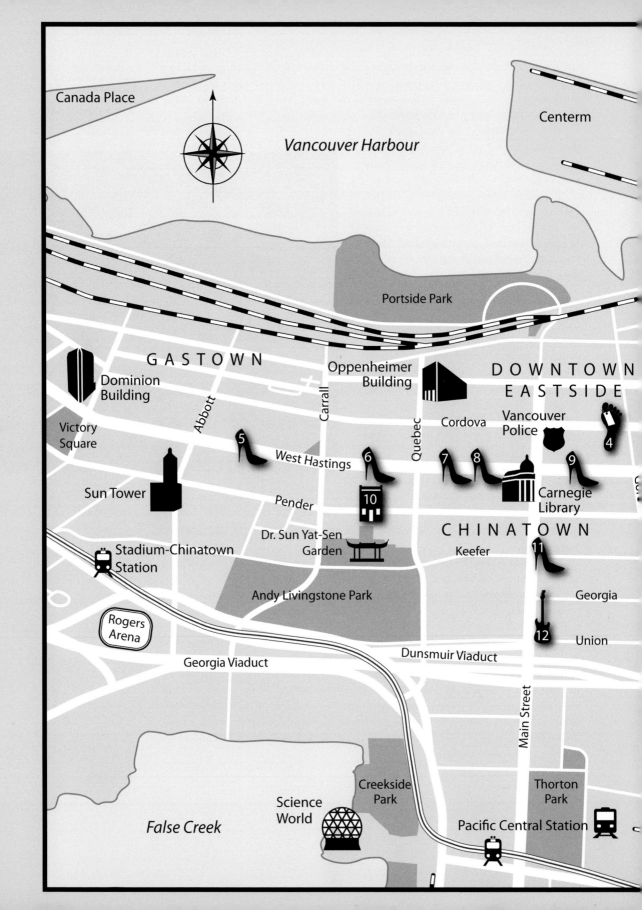

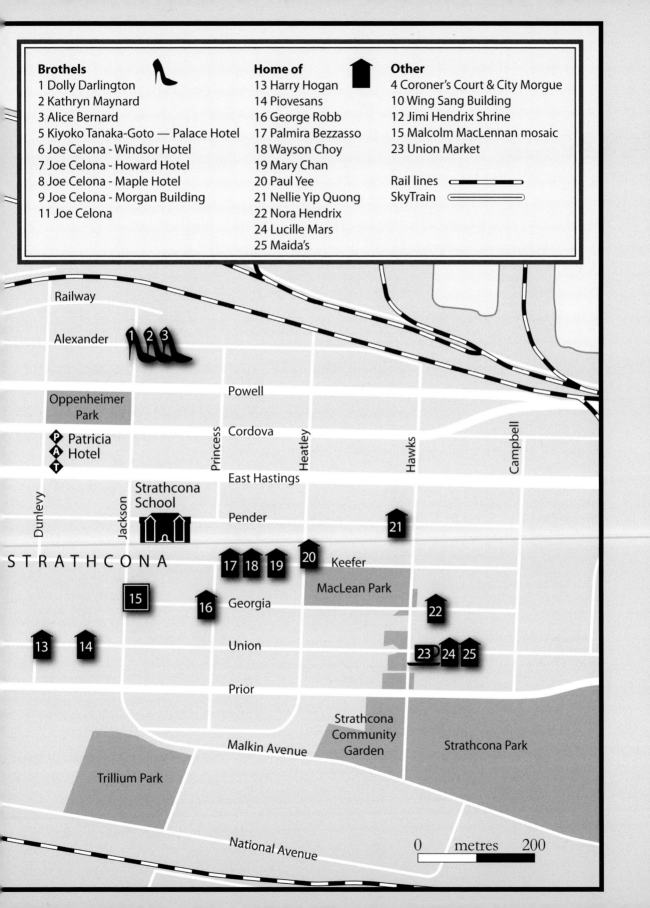

Brothels
1 Dolly Darlington
2 Kathryn Maynard
3 Alice Bernard
5 Kiyoko Tanaka-Goto — Palace Hotel
6 Joe Celona - Windsor Hotel
7 Joe Celona - Howard Hotel
8 Joe Celona - Maple Hotel
9 Joe Celona - Morgan Building
11 Joe Celona

Home of
13 Harry Hogan
14 Piovesans
16 George Robb
17 Palmira Bezzasso
18 Wayson Choy
19 Mary Chan
20 Paul Yee
21 Nellie Yip Quong
22 Nora Hendrix
24 Lucille Mars
25 Maida's

Other
4 Coroner's Court & City Morgue
10 Wing Sang Building
12 Jimi Hendrix Shrine
15 Malcolm MacLennan mosaic
23 Union Market

Rail lines
SkyTrain

Railway

Alexander

Powell

Oppenheimer
Park

Cordova

Princess

Heatley

Hawks

Campbell

Patricia
Hotel

East Hastings

Strathcona
School

Dunlevy

Jackson

Pender

21

S T R A T H C O N A

17 18 19

20

Keefer

MacLean Park

15

16

Georgia

22

13 14

Union

23 24 25

Prior

Strathcona
Community
Garden

Strathcona Park

Malkin Avenue

Trillium Park

National Avenue

0   metres   200

Bibliography

BOOKS

Ackery, Ivan. (1980). *Fifty Years on Theatre Row*. North Vancouver: Hancock House Publishers.

Atkin, John. (1994). *Strathcona: Vancouver's First Neighbourhood*. Vancouver: Whitecap Books.

Belshaw, John & Purvey, Diane. (2011). *Vancouver Noir: 1930-1960*. Vancouver: Anvil Press.

Bourgeois-Doyle, Richard. (2008). *Her Daughter the Engineer: The Life of Elsie Gregory MacGill*. Ottawa: NRC Research Press.

Bridge, Kathryn A. (2002). *Phyllis Munday: Mountaineer*. Sechelt: Harbour Publishing.

Bublé, Michael. (2011). *On Stage Off Stage: The Official Illustrated Memoir*. Toronto: Doubleday Canada.

Chong, Denise. (1997). *The Concubine's Children*. Toronto: Penguin Books.

Choy, Wayson. (1999). *Paper Shadows: A Chinatown Childhood*. Toronto: Viking Press.

Cooper, M.E. (2007). *Bold and Brassy: Oklahoma's own Black Widow*. Alex, OK: Padlock Mystery Press.

Culos, Raymond. (1998). *Vancouver's Society of Italians*. Sechelt: Harbour Publishing.

Davis, Chuck. (Ed.). (1997). *The Greater Vancouver Book*. Surrey: The Linkman Press.

Delgado, James P. (2003). *Racers and Rovers: 100 Years of the Royal Vancouver Yacht Club*. Vancouver: Douglas & McIntyre.

Forster, Merna. (2004). *100 Canadian Heroines: Famous and Forgotten Faces*. Toronto: The Dundurn Group.

Forster, Merna. (2011). *100 More Canadian Heroines: Famous and Forgotten Faces*. Toronto: The Dundurn Group.

Foster, Hamar & McLaren, John. (Eds.). (1995). *Essays in the History of Canadian Law: The Legal History of British Columbia and the Yukon*. Toronto: University of Toronto Press.

Francis, Daniel. (2004). *LD: Mayor Louis Taylor and the Rise of Vancouver*. Vancouver: Arsenal Pulp Press.

Francis, Daniel. (2006). *Red Light Neon: A History of Vancouver's Sex Trade*. Vancouver: Subway Books.

Greene, Ruth. (1969). *Personality Ships of British Columbia*. West Vancouver: Marine Tapestry Publications Ltd.

Holt, Simma. (2008). *Memoirs of a Loose Cannon*. Hamilton: Seraphim Editions.

Iglauer, Edith. (1981). *Seven Stones: A Portrait of Arthur Erickson, Architect*. Sechelt: Harbour Publishing.

Itter, Carole & Marlatt, Daphne. (1979). *Opening Doors: Vancouver's East End*. Sound Heritage Series, Vol. V11, nos. 1-2. Victoria: Aural History Program.

Kalman, Harold & Ward, Robin. (2012). *Exploring Vancouver: The Architectural Guide*. Vancouver: Douglas & McIntyre.

Keller, Betty. (1986). *On the Shady Side: Vancouver 1886-1914*. Ganges: Horsdal & Schubart.

King, James. (2012). *Inward Journey: The Life of Lawren Harris*. Toronto: Thomas Allen Publishers.

Kogawa, Joy. (1981). *Obasan*. Toronto: Penguin Canada.

Lawrence, Sharon. (2004). *Jimi Hendrix, the Man, the Magic, the Truth*. Toronto: Harper Entertainment.

Luxton, Donald (Ed.). (2003). *Building the West: The Early Architects of British Columbia*. Vancouver: Talonbooks.

Luxton, Donald & Associates. (1997). *The Modern Architecture of North Vancouver: 1930-1965*. North Vancouver: The Heritage Inventory of the District of North Vancouver.

Macdonald, Ian & O'Keefe, Betty. (1997). *The Mulligan Affair: Top Cop on the Take*. Victoria: Heritage House Publishing Company.

MacGill, Elsie G. (1955). *My Mother the Judge*. Toronto: The Ryerson Press.

Miles, Fraser. (1992). *Slow Boat on Rum Row*. Sechelt, BC: Harbour Publishing.

Munro, Raymond Z. (1985). *Sky's No Limit*. Toronto: Key Porter Books.

Nilsen, Deborah. (1976). *The Social Evil: Prostitution in Vancouver, 1900-1920.* Vancouver: University of British Columbia Press.

Petrie, Blair. (1995). *Mole Hill Living Heritage.* Vancouver: Living Heritage Society.

Rogatnick, Abraham J. & Thom, Ian M. & Weder, A. (2006). *B.C. Binning.* Vancouver: Douglas & McIntyre.

Shadbolt, Douglas. (1995). *Ron Thom: The Shaping of an Architect.* Vancouver: Douglas & McIntyre.

Spaner, David. (2003). *Dreaming in the Rain: How Vancouver Became Hollywood North.* Vancouver: Arsenal Press.

Stone, Jim. (2002). *My Dad the Rum Runner.* North Waterloo: Academic Press.

Swan, Joe. (1986). *A Century of Service: The Vancouver Police 1886-1986.* Vancouver: Vancouver Police Historical Society and Centennial Museum.

Swan, Joe. (1991). *Police Beat: 24 Vancouver Murders.* Vancouver: Cosmopolitan Publishing Company.

Varley, Peter. (1983). *Frederick H. Varley.* Toronto: Key Porter Books.

Watanabe, Kiriko & Weder, Adele & Luxton, Donald & Downs, Barry. (2012). *Selwyn Pullan: Photographing Mid-Century West Coast Modernism.* Vancouver: Douglas & McIntyre.

Webster, Jack. (1990). *Webster!* Vancouver: Douglas & McIntyre.

Williams, David R. (1986). *Mayor Gerry: The Remarkable Gerald Grattan McGeer.* Vancouver: Douglas & McIntyre.

Windover, Michael. (2012). *Art Deco: a mode of mobility.* Quebec: Presses de L'Université du Quebec.

WEBSITES

abcbookworld.com

bcassessment.ca

conservancy.bc.ca

genealogysearch.org/Canada/british-columbia.html

greatestates.info

historicplaces.ca

pasttensevancouver.wordpress.com

vancouverhistory.ca

vancouver Public Library, city directories: vpl.ca/bccd/index.php

thesailingchannel.tv

NEWSPAPERS & PERIODICALS

BC Federationist (1912)
Coquitlam Now
Delta Optimist
Flash (1955)
North Shore News
Province
Quill and Quire
The Standard
Time Colonist
The Truth (1912)
Vancouver Sun
Vancouver Courier

GOVERNMENT SOURCES

Vancouver Police Inquiry 1928: R.S. Lennie Esq., Commission.

Final Report of the Vancouver City Police Force Inquiry, June 24, 1955. R.H. Tupper, QC., Commissioner. February 17, 1956

VANCOUVER POLICE MUSEUM

Halliday, Carolyn. Speech given at the International Association of Women Police--Many Minnies Later, 1995. Vancouver Police Museum.

Vancouver Police Department, Annual Reports, 1906, 1911-1918, 1920, 1921, 1929, 1930

Detective Report Books (1901-1985)

Prisoner Record Books (1912-1913)

Historic clippings (1907/08)

Coast Modern documentary, 2012

Index